DUE

OFF-SEASON
TRAINING

for cyclists

*by Edmund R. Burke, Ph.D.
with Harvey Newton, M.A.*

VELO
press

BOULDER, COLORADO USA

International Standard Book Number: 1-884737-40-4

Library of Congress Cataloging-in-Publication applied for.

PRINTED IN THE USA

Design by Erin Johnson

10 9 8 7 6 5 4 3 2

VELO
press

1830 N. 55th Street • Boulder, Colorado • 80301-2700 • USA
303/440-0601 • FAX 303/444-6788 • E-MAIL velopress@7dogs.com

To purchase additional copies of this book or other Velo products,
call 800/234-8356 or visit us on the Web at www.velocatalogue.com

DISCLAIMER

The information and ideas in this book are for educational and instructional purposes and are not intended as prescriptive advice. Consult your physician before starting any exercise program, especially if you have been sedentary for several years, are over the age of 35, have a history of heart disease, or have any other medical condition that may require consultation before beginning a training program.

A C K N O W L E D G M E N T S

I would like to thank VeloPress, which saw the need to produce a much-needed book on off-season training for cyclists. I am especially indebted to Patrick O'Grady for his fine editing and comments on cyclo-cross, and Amy Sorrells, whose support, encouragement, and, when necessary, prodding, helped me finish this project; to Harvey Newton, for his insight and guidance on resistance-training exercises specifically designed for the cyclist; and to Arnie Baker for his stationary-cycling plans. And finally, thanks to Schwinn Cycling & Fitness for the use of its equipment for photographs.

TABLE OF CONTENTS

FOREWORD

The purpose of this book is to introduce you to off-season and indoor training with the goal of improving your in-season cycling performance. This book will help you construct an off-season training program tailored to your particular needs and interests.

The preparation of this book was an exciting challenge. When approached by VeloPress to produce a book on off-season training, I called upon my years of experience and many hours of working with competitive athletes to put together the best possible book for the cycling competitor and enthusiast. I have also written this book for those who are contemplating their first investment in indoor conditioning equipment, as well as those who already know something about such devices but need a useful handbook for setting up a comprehensive program.

Research indicates that lack of motivation is the major reason people don't get as much out of indoor exercise or strength training as they should. Knowing this, I have provided easy-to-follow guidelines for designing an off-season fitness program. I have also included detailed instructions and illustrations on how to use the various pieces of equipment and easy-to-read charts for interpreting your results.

As you read *Off-Season Training for Cyclists*, keep in mind that becoming knowledgeable about off-season and cross-training is only one of the essential ingredients in your personal recipe for a sensible yearly training program.

To make your off-season experience as productive and enjoyable as possible, you need to take several steps. Undoubtedly, the most critical is to make an unwavering commitment to regular exercise. For most individuals, that commitment will be based, at least in part, on an understanding that activities listed in this book make sense for any cyclist who is looking for a break from the bicycle and wants a stronger body for the upcoming season.

Explore this book. Use it as a reference, or read it page by page. And good luck as you begin using these suggestions to augment your cycling program.

Edmund R. Burke, Ph.D.
Colorado Springs, Colorado

why Should you Cross-train?

Cross-training \kros-tran-ing\ *n* 1: a form of conditioning stressing the use of multiple activities for achieving total body fitness; 2: an anger-management technique developed by Esalen Institute; 3: a marketing program developed by Nike to sell more shoes.

You trained hard throughout the season, and now you want a little rest. You don't even want to think about serious cycling, not even if the weather permits it. It's the off-season — time to call it quits until spring, right?

Wrong.

After a short break, which is necessary for recovery, consider doing some cross-training during the off-season — mountain biking on snow, stair-stepping or rowing at your health club, cross-country skiing or snowshoeing, running, or strength training.

The idea behind off-season training is to integrate other activities with your cycling skills — activities that will increase your strength, power and endurance. It's a great feeling to get back on the bike come springtime with last season's fitness intact, and perhaps even enhanced, without the potential for

1

burnout that comes from cycling year-round.

Cross-training emphasizes comprehensive conditioning. This is not a new concept. For years, many cyclists have sought a total-body workout during the off-season, employing such off-the-bike activities as running, lifting weights, skiing and swimming.

Cross-training relieves boredom, helps prevent injuries, lets you maintain fitness during recovery from injury, and makes exercising during the off-season more enjoyable.

By developing and maintaining a sensible cross-training program, you can:

• *Strike a balance between cardiovascular conditioning, strength, coordination and flexibility.* Participation in a variety of activities helps recruit new muscle fibers and develops new neuromuscular pathways. The results can include increases in aerobic capacity, muscular strength and endurance, and total-body flexibility.

The new challenges and overloads afforded by cross-training allows one to work more, and differently. If your cycling program has stalled, this can give you the motivation to get it going again.

• *Achieve comprehensive cardio-respiratory conditioning.* Cross-training is one of the most powerful techniques available to achieve total-body fitness and health. The aerobic portion of a cross-training program can improve the efficiency of the heart and lungs.

• *Enhance your muscular balance.* Many cyclists are becoming more aware of the importance of muscle symmetry — the appropriate balance between strength and flexibility in opposing muscle groups. Overworking one muscle group allows it to become too strong and its opposing muscles disproportionally weak. Well-balanced muscle pairs, working in concert, allow for more effective and efficient movement, and may decrease injuries. Cross-training allows for greater muscle symmetry.

• *Find your off-season exercise more exciting and challenging.* Studies of exercise adherence indicate that burnout or boredom has ended many an exercise program. As the saying goes, "Variety is the spice of life." Cross-training, with its variety of challenges, can stimulate your motivation as much as your musculature during the long winter months.

WHAT ABOUT SPECIFICITY?

The cross-training concept finds itself in direct opposition to a traditional principle of sport called "specificity of training." This concept implies that sport movements and training are specific to one sport and do not improve performance in another sport.

This form of training overloads the exact muscles involved in a specific activity, in a specific way. An athlete who wants to be a competitive road cyclist must ride long distances; swimming, rowing or playing basketball are not acceptable substitutes for on-the-bike training.

However, off-season activities such as power hiking, stair-stepping, interval training on a Spinning® Bike and in-line skating will have solid carry-over value for cycling by improving the performance of the heart, lungs and blood. Some strength training, meanwhile, will increase the cyclist's overall strength,

3

and may reduce injuries.

If you are a mountain biker, alpine skiing may help you achieve greater power, balance and total-body awareness. Road cyclists can use mountain biking to increase their bike-handling skills. Running and tumbling exercises can help you survive a crash with minimal damage. Yoga can increase your flexibility.

With this book, and a little imagination, a great workout is only a few moments away. All it may take is a different grip on the multi-gym, a varied rhythm on the stair-stepper, a group indoor ride on a Spinning® Bike at your local club, or a long workout in the woods on snowshoes or cross-country skis. Keep varying your workout menu and you'll make the most gains in the least time.

A well-designed and varied off-season training program will allow you to reach your fitness goals while properly preparing you for the upcoming cycling season.

Let's begin with an examination of the benefits of strength training.

CHAPTER TWO

Strength Training
for cyclists

"Cycling takes so many hours to train and so many years to be really strong. Being good at cycling doesn't happen because you train hard one year." — *Rune Hoydahl, Professional mountain biker*

Successful performance in cycling requires a combination of muscular strength, power and endurance. Strength is the ability to overcome an external force, such as your foot against a pedal. Power is the ability to overcome the external force in the shortest amount of time. And the quickest and surest way to achieve both strength and power is through strength training.

Both strength and power stress the anaerobic energy system, which is *not* dependent on oxygen. Endurance is the ability to sustain an activity for a longer time. This works the aerobic energy system, which *is* dependent on oxygen.

When you are working your muscles intensely for short periods, such as lifting weights or sprinting on the bike, you

5

emphasize your anaerobic energy system. When you are working your muscles moderately for a long period, such as during a long training ride, you emphasize your aerobic energy system. This improves your aerobic capacity, or VO_2 max, which is the ability to use oxygen to produce work. Success at cycling demands a combination of both aerobic and anaerobic energy systems.

The particular event for which a cyclist trains determines which system needs emphasis in training. Mountain-bike racing requires mostly muscular endurance, which is the ability to maintain a high force on the pedals for a long time, but also demands power for climbing steep hills and sprinting for the finish line. The same holds true for road racing, for which you need endurance for covering long miles on a day-to-day basis, and power to sprint at the end of a race. The match sprint on the track depends primarily on strength for starts and power for a short, explosive effort, though endurance is important for the long training days.

In general, cyclists train adequately for endurance. But to build strength and power, they need strength training.

THE BENEFITS OF STRENGTH TRAINING

Strength training can improve your athletic performance and overall health in many ways. Its greatest benefit is helping you maintain lean body mass as you grow older. As the saying goes, "You either use it, or lose it."

But strength training also offers two benefits that are extremely important for any endurance athlete: improved aerobic performance, and injury prevention.

IMPROVED AEROBIC PERFORMANCE

Strength training has become a hot topic of discussion among scientists, trainers, coaches and athletes. Are strength training and aerobic conditioning compatible during the same conditioning periods? Will strength training improve power, suppleness, endurance and speed in the same way, or perhaps better than, cycling without strength training?

To many, it doesn't seem logical that strength training, a predominantly anaerobic activity, can improve cycling, which is predominantly aerobic. But it appears that research supports this hypothesis.

Why? Because while your primary "engine" during exercise at a comfortable pace is the aerobic energy system, when you are starting to push the pace, or approaching the end of a long ride, the anaerobic energy system becomes more important. If you have honed your anaerobic energy system through strength training, you will be able to ride harder and faster before fatigue sets in.

Generally, exercise scientists did not expect strength training to affect VO_2 max, since lifting weights does not stress the aerobic energy system. But several recently published studies and books have shown that strength training can increase both strength and time to exhaustion *without* increasing VO_2 max.

One study in the late 1980s investigated the effects of using heavy strength training to increase leg strength in eight runners and cyclists who had already trained for several years. The subjects strength-trained three days per week for 10 weeks, while continuing their normal endurance work.

After the 10 weeks of strength training, running time to

7

exhaustion at maximal work rates increased by 13 percent in the runners and 11 percent in the cyclists. Leg strength increased an average of 30 percent, with no increase in VO_2 max. Apparently as a result of their increased strength, the athletes were able to exercise longer before becoming fatigued.

The data did not demonstrate any negative performance effects of adding heavy strength-training workouts to endurance-training programs. The study suggests that certain types of endurance performance, particularly those requiring the recruitment of powerful, fast-twitch muscle fibers, are improved by strength training.

Edward Marcinik, Ph.D., and coworkers from the University of Maryland investigated the effects of strength training on lactate threshold and endurance performance. Eighteen healthy males were randomly assigned to either a strength-training group or to a control group who did not strength train (a standard of comparison for verifying the results of a research study) for 12 weeks.

There were no changes in either group's aerobic capacity after the 12 weeks. But the group that participated in strength training showed a 33 percent increase in cycling time to exhaustion at 75 percent of aerobic capacity which is about the intensity of a long, moderately difficult ride. In other words, the strength-training group was able to perform more work before fatigue set in.

There was also a significant reduction in plasma lactate concentrations at all exercise intensities between 55 and 75 percent of aerobic capacity. This reduction in the level of lactate, a by-product of exercise which is one cause of fatigue, suggests that strength training improved the efficiency of the anaerobic energy system. After the 12 weeks of resistance training, endurance performance also was associated with a 12-percent increase in lactate threshold, also known as the anaerobic threshold.

Steve Fleck, Ph.D., a strength and conditioning specialist who works with many elite athletes, says this study shows that a higher lactate threshold means that an athlete can ride at a higher intensity before fatigue sets in and causes a reduction in cycling speed.

"Their findings indicate that strength training improves endurance performance independently of changes in oxygen consumption," Fleck says. "This improvement appears to be related to increases in lactate threshold and increased leg strength." So it seems that strength training and endurance training are not mutually exclusive.

INJURY PREVENTION

Strength training not only improves strength and power and overall aerobic performance, it also prevents injuries. Strength training strengthens the muscles, tendons and ligaments around the foot, ankle, knee and hip joints. This corrects muscle imbalances and helps prevent post-race stiffness, aches and pains while lessening the chances of injury.

Muscle imbalance is common in cyclists, who typically have disproportionately strong legs but weak backs, shoulders and arms. This imbalance may lead to injury. The upper body needs strength training to balance the strong lower body and leg muscles also need balancing. Strength training translates into real advantages for any type of cyclist, advantages that improve pedaling performance, endurance and speed.

MUSCULAR OR MUSCLE-BOUND?

While the need for increased strength in cycling is evident, most arguments against the use of strength training center on the premise that riders will become muscle-bound — hypertrophied — and gain too much weight.

Certainly, a cyclist does not want to carry useless weight. However, the type of strength-training program outlined in this book will actually help you climb and sprint more effectively without providing unnecessary bulk

Muscle growth depends to a large degree upon specific training and dietary regimens. If you concentrate on strengthening muscles specific to cycling, rather than becoming an Olympic-style weight lifter or body-builder, you shouldn't have any problems.

TERMINOLOGY

Before discussing the details of strength training, it is important to understand some basic terminology:

REPETITIONS (REPS) The number of times a weight is lifted consecutively.

SET A group of repetitions performed in sequence; a brief period of rest follows each set in order to recover.

REPETITION MAXIMUM (RM) The maximum number of reps you can handle for a specific weight. For instance, a 10 RM weight in the leg curl might be 40 pounds. This means you can perform 10 reps, but will fail to lift 40 pounds on the 11th rep.

NUMBER OF REPS

It is essential to understand the logic behind the number

of reps you will perform. Simply put, the number of reps you perform in a set will determine the benefits you derive from the exercise.

FIFTEEN OR MORE REPS: IMPROVED MUSCULAR ENDURANCE This number of reps is helpful during the first few weeks of strength training, but should not be used for an extended period of time. Generally speaking, cyclists get most of their muscular-endurance benefits on the bike, and should use resistance training for strengthening.

EIGHT TO 12 REPS: HYPERTROPHY, OR MUSCULAR GROWTH Performing reps in this range does not necessarily mean that you will get larger muscles. Such muscle growth is dependent on several factors, such as genetic potential, diet and amount of exercise. Cyclists should not be concerned that this will create the kind of muscle hypertrophy seen in body builders.

ONE TO SIX REPS: QUICK STRENGTH GAINS There is no need to "max out" by performing one, two or three RM movements. Such high-intensity attempts may lead to injury, especially for cyclists who are just beginning a strength-training program.

PERIODIZATION

Planned variety and purposeful training are the missing links in most cycling strength programs. Varying the sets, repetitions, loads and routines throughout the year produces the greatest results. This is known as "periodization."

During a season of on-the-bike training, cyclists will work at different levels of exertion at different times. During early season rides, it is common to train in the small chain ring, maintaining a rapid cadence — 90-100 rpm — at relatively low intensities. However, if cyclists trained this way all year long, they would be unable to meet the intense demands of cycling, which often requires using much larger gears with frequent accelerations, sprinting and hill climbs. As a result, on-bike training gradually increases the emphasis on high-intensity efforts.

In the same manner, strength training progresses from low to high intensity. If you always train at 10 or 15 reps, you will miss much of the strength benefit of resistance training. Strength comes from higher intensity and fewer reps. However, such high-intensity training should only be done after proper preparation — lifting lighter weights at higher repetitions.

The exception to this involves the novice weight lifter. In your first year of strength training, you should concentrate on learning the proper technique of the exercises, working in the eight-to 12-repetition range. After the first year, use the periodized approach described here.

There are five phases to the periodized strength-training program. They are Transition, Foundation, Strength, Power and Maintenance.

Transition Period

The season is over, and you've taken a few weeks of "active rest," which means you put the bike away and turned to other forms of aerobic training to maintain fitness. For most cyclists this would be sometime during the month of October. This period is essential, since it helps prevent both physical and mental "burnout." The days are also shorter and colder, and you may be forced to train indoors.

At this time of year, resistance training begins with the Transition phase — a change in emphasis, from cycling to strength training. This phase, which lasts two to four weeks, prepares you for the higher-intensity strength training that comes later. Just as you ease back into training on the bike, you need to ease into strength training. The purpose is to get started correctly, without experiencing unnecessary muscle soreness.

In many cases, the exercises may involve using only your body weight, rather than lifting external loads at a club or on a home gym. Body-weight exercises could include push-ups, pull-ups, crunches, floor back extensions and lunges. If you find upper body exercises such as push-ups and pull-ups too difficult to perform for the assigned number of reps, use a home gym to perform exercises that work the same muscles in a similar fashion.

The Transition phase uses either circuit or priority training. Circuit training means performing Set 1 of Exercise A, resting briefly, moving immediately to Set 1 of Exercise B, resting briefly, then completing Set 1 of Exercise C, and so on, until you have performed one set of each exercise.

The exercise sequence is varied so that emphasis is not maintained on a particular part of the body, and blood flow is constantly changing. Circuit training produces good cardio-respiratory benefits, and many cyclists prefer it. However, because rest is minimal between exercises, and because exercises vary greatly, the standard benefits of strength training — strength, power and muscular growth — are minimal. Circuit training is recommended for the Transition phase.

In priority training, you perform Set 1 of Exercise A, rest one

13

to two minutes, perform Set 2 of Exercise A, rest one to two minutes, and perform Set 3 of Exercise A. Then you rest and continue in the same manner with Exercise B. This is the normally recommended mode of strength training.

With priority training, it is important to get off the exercise apparatus and move around between sets. Get a drink of water, record your workout in a training log or cheer on your training partner during your break. You will recover and come back ready for another hard effort on the next set, as opposed to circuit training, in which the rest is designed to be inadequate before another hard effort.

In the Transition phase, repetitions range from 12 to 20 with one to three sets. Resistance is light to moderate and the exercises used will be general in nature combining both upper and lower body exercises. This phase is similar to your first easy-spinning, low-geared outdoor rides in the winter.

Foundation

High volume is the key to this phase, which usually falls during the months of November and December. Weights are moderate, with eight to 12 reps in three to five sets.

The Foundation phase is important because you are preparing the muscles for the hard work ahead. It coincides with the long, slow distance mileage of the early season. In both cases, the volume is high and the intensity is moderate. This phase may last four to six weeks.

Basic Strength

As the name implies, the object of this phase is to get

strong. Training loads increase, with five to seven sets of two to six reps each. Before lifting heavy weights, it is essential to have a proper warm-up, performing the same movement with lighter weights.

The Basic Strength phase is similar to adding hill work to your riding. Injury is more likely if you begin with this phase before doing the Transition and Foundation phases. However, by following the proper phases, your muscles will be prepared for this heavy load. This phase lasts four to six weeks, during the months of December and January.

Power

Strength by itself is fine, but to ensure success as a cyclist you want explosive force. Explosive force improves your sprint and climbing of short, "power" hills. The objective of the Power phase is the creation of power on the bike. This combination of speed and strength is probably the most important benefit of strength training for cycling.

Since power is the ability to apply force quickly, the main emphasis in the Power phase is on speed of movement. During this phase, the actual lifting motion should be performed more rapidly than in the other phases, while the recovery portion of the movement remains slow and controlled.

The Power phase lasts at least four weeks, and perhaps as long as six weeks, during the months of January and February. Since it is late winter or early spring and you are riding more, it is acceptable to cut your strength training back to two days per week for this phase. Weights and sets are reduced somewhat, with three to six sets of four to 15 reps.

Maintenance

Finally, the racing season has arrived, and you may be doing all your riding outdoors. Now, you must decide whether to continue strength training.

Usually it is wise to maintain some strength work, especially in body parts like the abdominals, arms and back, which do not get much of a workout while cycling. You can maintain your strength with minimal training.

The Maintenance phase includes two workouts each week, lasting 20 to 30 minutes each. Circuit training is suggested, as this will further develop muscular endurance. And your strength-training workouts should be tapered from seven to 10 days before a major event, like a race or century, in order to emphasize cycling.

This year-round, periodized training approach is a healthy and proper training regimen that will help prepare you for any major event or simply keep you fit and strong. The following chart outlines the five phases involved in periodized strength training.

STRENGTH TRAINING PHASES

PHASE	BENEFIT	DAYS/WK	SETS	REPS	WEIGHT	LENGTH
Transition	preparation	3	1-3	12-20	light to moderate	2-4 wks
Foundation	muscle growth	3	3-5	8-12	moderate	4-6 wks
Basic Strength	strength	3	5-7	2-6	heavy	4-6 wks
Power	explosive force	2-3	3-6	4-15	moderate with speed	4-6 wks
Maintenance	maintain	2	1-2	4-8	moderate	season

JUMP FOR STRENGTH WITH PLYOMETRICS

Another strength-training program that many cyclists use is called plyometrics. Plyometrics, simply defined, is a series of drills that places muscles in a stretched position before they shorten (concentric contraction). The results are said to be improved strength, speed and explosive power.

Plyometric movements such as jumping rope, bench hops and bounding have put cyclists on the road to increased strength and speed for at least a quarter-century. The information in this section will help you design a simple plyometric program for the off-season.

Research into plyometrics and muscle physiology shows that a muscle will contract more forcefully and quickly from a pre-stretched position; the more rapid the pre-stretch, the more forceful the concentric contraction.

Plyometric movements combine an eccentric (muscle-lengthening) phase with an explosive-concentric (muscle-shortening) phase to pre-stretch muscles before they shorten during contraction.

Picture a rubber band and how it responds to stretching. Then think of the muscles as a structure of contractile and elastic components. (Both help in the development of muscular force.) The elastic component can be stretched, thereby developing tension due to its elastic resistance to that stretch. Again, think of stretching a rubber band. As you increase the stretch on the band, the tension and velocity of shortening is also increased.

Muscles have receptors that are sensitive to stretching. When a muscle lengthens quickly, a reflex causes the muscle to contract. Inducing this stretch reflex in conjunction with the volun-

17

tary muscle contraction results in a more vigorous contraction.

Plyometric training overloads the muscles via jumping movements. When you land from a jump (see illustration on page 65), the muscles tense while lengthening to a stretched position (eccentric contraction). This is followed immediately by an explosive concentric contraction (another jump). The goal is to simulate the movements and speed of contraction used in competition.

Research has shown that plyometrics increases strength and power. In a study with collegiate football players, one group used plyometric drills (jumping from a height of 45 cm) in combination with weight training. A control group did only conventional weight training exercises. After six weeks the group using plyometrics had greater gains in strength.

In another study, subjects used a jumping height of 34 inches and gradually added weight (with a weight vest) up to 20 pounds. After eight weeks there was an increase of more than 2 inches in vertical jump, a 10-percent improvement.

Plyometrics can be used like weight training, applying the overload principle by progressively increasing the number of repetitions, the number of sets, the height of the jumping block, and the weight in the weight vest. As with any training program, the athlete's age must be considered. A mature cyclist can usually handle such rigorous workouts. A Senior category cyclist (18 years or older) can probably use plyometrics year-round, while a Junior should use it only in the off-season.

You should be careful not to overload the thigh muscles, which may lead to knee pain. Use progressive resistance (higher/deeper or longer jumps) and don't overstrain your muscles.

Plyometrics is best suited to cyclists who need to develop power, speed and acceleration. Those who compete in the kilometer, match sprint, pursuit and downhill mountain bike race can expect significant improvement from a progressive plyometric program. The long-distance road specialist may wish to use it only in the off-season, if he or she has a poor ability to accelerate quickly or "jump" in a sprint.

During the first three weeks, limit your workout to broad jumps, bounce jumps, single-leg hops, and jumps off low boxes. Work out twice a week, doing no more than 60 jumping movements (repetitions) per session.

After three weeks, increase the sessions to every other day and the repetitions to 75-85. Incorporate a variety of hopping exercises into your program. For example, hop first on your right leg, then on your left, as you would in exaggerated running. Or try right, right, left, left, or all right leg or all left. Do these hops for 30 yards at full speed. Add jumps from boxes 14-24 inches high. This phase should last about four weeks.

After a month you can increase the height of the boxes (no more than 36 inches) and wear a weight vest. Don't use ankle weights — they're too hard on the feet and ankles. This is when you add depth jumps to the program as described in Chapter Three under "Advanced Plyometrics." The maximum number of repetitions per workout should be 100 total.

Once the racing season arrives, you can continue to do one or two plyometric sessions per week, depending on your needs. For example, a kilometer rider, sprinter and downhill mountain biker would do more days per week during the season leading up to his or her major competition, whereas a pursuiter may only do one day a week and remove all plyometric drills from his or her program in the last two to three weeks before a major competition.

Specific instructions on performing plyometric jumps and a suggested program will be outlined in Chapter Three.

SUMMARY

As you strengthen the muscles used in cycling, you will become a better cyclist. You will climb hills with greater authority, and hammer on the flats with greater endurance. Most important, you will make the time you spend on your bicycle more enjoyable and comfortable.

Strength Training
Exercises

"Machines don't break records. Muscles do."
— Lon Haldeman,
Ultra-marathon cyclist

Now that you have an understanding of how your strength training should proceed throughout the year, it's time to study the exercises in detail.

Strength training can be done in a number of ways: using the weight-stack machinery at your health club; on a home multi-gym; with free weights using a weight bench and squat rack; without equipment, using plyometrics; or in some combination of these.

Begin by dividing your strength workout into the following six categories:

- Upper-body pushing.
- Upper-body pulling.
- Lower back.
- Abdominals.
- Lower body.
- Supplemental or specialty exercises.

Exercises for each category are listed below. When designing your workout, pick at least one exercise from each of the first five. Add one or two exercises from the sixth; pick the ones you think will benefit you the most. Next, determine the number of sets and reps you will perform. Finally, determine how much weight you can lift in each set. Your first set should be a warm-up — the weight used should be 50 percent of what you can lift in your last set.

PROGRESSIVE RESISTANCE

If your strength training is to be successful, it must incorporate the principle of progressive resistance. This means that you must regularly strive to improve your best record in a particular movement for an assigned number of reps.

Once you can consistently perform more than one set for the assigned number of reps, you should increase the load in your next workout. This is how you gain strength. You probably will need to decrease the number of reps you can perform until your body adapts to the new load.

Just as you would not expect to make improvements on your bike by always riding the same course, in the same gear, at the same speed, you should not continue to lift the same weight for the same number of reps and sets.

Chart 3.1 illustrates progressive strength training for the chest press.

Once you have devised your training menu, do your strength workouts three times per week, with one day of rest from weight-lifting between each workout. Monday, Wednesday and Friday are recommended.

3.1 Progressive strength training: chest press

Date: Week of 10/3	Set 1	Set 2	Set 3
Weight/reps	40/15	60/12	80/10
notes: increase reps			
Date: Week of 10/10	Set 1	Set 2	Set 3
Weight/reps	40/15	60/14	80/13
notes: increase reps			
Date: Week of 10/17	Set 1	Set 2	Set 3
Weight/reps	40/15	60/15	80/15
notes: increase weight			
Date: Week of 10/24	Set 1	Set 2	Set 3
Weight/reps	45/12	70/12	90/10
notes: increase reps			
Date: Week of 11/1	Set 1	Set 2	Set 3
Weight/reps	45/13	70/13	90/11
notes: increase reps			
Date: Week of 11/8	Set 1	Set 2	Set 3
Weight/reps	45/15	70/15	90/12

TRAINING WITH A WEIGHT-STACK MACHINE

Each strength-training exercise listed below includes explanations of how to position your body relative to the equipment; the exercise movement pattern; how the exercise may directly benefit your cycling; and the muscles involved.

If you are considering purchasing home strength equipment, when should you consider choosing weight-stack machines? When space is limited and you do not have anyone to spot you during lifting. Most weight-stack machines give you an impressive amount of equipment per square foot compared to free weights. A well-designed home gym will require approximately 50- to 70-square feet of floor space. Achieving the same workout using free weights and the necessary benches and racks could require up to 100-square feet or more.

Availability is the deciding factor for many exercisers. Weight-stack machines allow you to complete a workout in very little time, since placing plates on a barbell or dumbbell and moving benches and racks is eliminated from your program. Another major consideration for those working out at home is safety. Most multi-station gyms eliminate the need for spotters — not to mention the possibility of dropping the weight to the floor.

The biggest advance in home gyms the last few years has come in their improved design. Many of the home gym's exercises are as effective as those performed on a more expensive piece of single-station equipment at most health clubs. This is even more impressive when you consider that one piece of health-club equipment could cost as much as your whole home gym.

The background research on this type of equipment actually begins in your own home. First, make sure the ceiling is high enough to accommodate the unit you're thinking about purchasing. If you are really tight for space, consider a machine that offers a vertical bench press and a standing leg curl instead of a prone curl.

And remember that you get what you pay for in home gyms. Most lower-priced, multi-station machines may not offer good-quality components, be biomechanically designed and stable, and have the feel of a higher-priced unit. Conversely, do not over-buy. A higher-priced machine may be too much equipment for your needs. The money you save could be spent on a treadmill or stationary bike.

UPPER-BODY-PUSHING EXERCISES

Upper-body-pushing exercises include some form of elbow extension, or straightening of the elbow joint. We all know how fatigued we feel early in the season, especially after a long ride. This fatigue usually shows up in the hands, the triceps (back of the upper arms), the trapezius muscles (upper back), and the neck muscles.

Upper-body pushing may not help you ride any faster, but it will help develop a well-rounded, total-body strength that can make your riding easier. Increased upper-body strength is particularly important to those specializing in mountain biking, where greater strength is required to control the bike, and for the majority of women cyclists, who tend to have less upper-body strength than men.

Recommended exercises include:
- Chest press.
- Triceps extension.
- Triceps pushdown.

Chest press

PREPARATION Sit at chest press station with back against pad and handles at shoulder level. Release lock lever and fit roll pads to top hole for leg room if required.

DESCRIPTION From the seated position, grip handles and push forward by extending the elbows. Keep shoulders and

[CHEST PRESS]

hips in place and do not arch the low back.

CYCLING APPLICATION Upper-body support while riding and overall balance of muscularity/strength.

MUSCLES Deltoids, triceps and pectorals.

Triceps extension

PREPARATION Fit T-bar or sraps to pulley. Grab strap on pulley behind head.

DESCRIPTION Use a narrow grip, with palms facing upward (pronated). Keep elbows close together and pointed upward. Bend and extend the elbow joint in a smooth motion, being sure to allow the bar to come all the way down. Completely straighten the arms at the top.

CYCLING APPLICATION Support upper body, especially while on handlebar drops.

MUSCLES Triceps.

[TRICEPS EXTENSION]

[TRICEPS PUSHDOWN]

Triceps pushdown

PREPARATION Fit T-bar to high pulley. Adjust the chain to chest height.

DESCRIPTION Place hands about three inches apart, with palms facing downward. Keep your elbows alongside your

27

torso throughout the entire movement and straighten the elbow joint until your arm is straight. Slowly return to starting position (elbow fully bent).

CYCLING APPLICATION Support of upper body, especially while on handlebar drops.

MUSCLES Triceps.

UPPER-BODY-PULLING EXERCISES

Upper-body-pulling exercises involve some form of elbow flexion, or bending of the elbow joint. The upper body is particularly important in its contribution to added strength and power in climbing hills or in sprinting.

Recommended exercises include:

- Lat-machine pulldown.
- Low rowing.

[LAT MACHINE PULLDOWN]

- Arm curl.
- Upright rowing.

Lat-machine pulldown

PREPARATION Fit lat bar to high pulley and roll pads to top hole. Sit on bench with thighs secured by upper roll pads. Torso should be four to six inches in front of back pad.

DESCRIPTION Grip handles with an over-hand (pronated) grip,

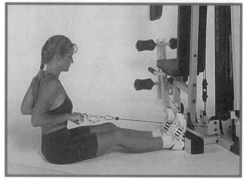

[LOW ROWING]

using narrow, medium or wide grip. Be sure arms stretch fully over head. Pull the bar down until bar touches upper back. Slowly return to starting position.

CYCLING APPLICATION Upper-body support while on handle-bars, overall balance of body muscularity/strength and pulling on bars while climbing.

MUSCLES Latissimus dorsi, biceps, rhomboids and pectorals.

Low rowing

PREPARATION Fit foot brace and slide it out as far as possible. Fit bar with chain to low pulley and adjust length.

DESCRIPTION Keep back flat, and knees slightly bent throughout the lift. Grip the bar at shoulder width. From a fully

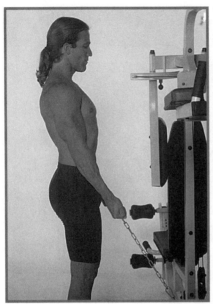

[ARM CURL]

extended arm position, bend the elbows and pull bar until it touches the lower chest or upper abdomen. Slowly return to starting position.

CYCLING APPLICATION Pulling on the bars during sprints or climbing.

MUSCLES Latissimus dorsi, biceps brachii and posterior deltoid.

Arm curl

PREPARATION Fit foot brace in middle position. Fit T-bar and chain to low pulley. Adjust length so arms can fully extend in the lowered position. Stand on foot brace.

DESCRIPTION Grip the bar with palms up (supinated). Arms are straight and elbows in contact with torso. Slowly bend the elbows and wrists to "curl" the bar to a position touching the neck.

CYCLING APPLICATION Sprinting, hill climbing and any

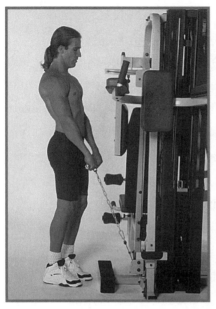

[UPRIGHT ROWING]

pulling motion on the handlebars.

MUSCLES Biceps and other elbow flexors.

Upright rowing

PREPARATION Fit foot brace and T-bar to low pulley with chain. Adjust length so that arms can fully extend in the lowered position.

DESCRIPTION Grip the bar with index fingers about four inches apart and palms facing body (pronated). Pull up by bending elbows. Keep the bar as close to the body as possible and pull until the bar is under the chin. Elbows should be higher than the bar throughout the entire movement. Slowly return to the starting position.

CYCLING APPLICATION Sprinting, hill climbing and any pulling motion on the handlebars.

MUSCLES Biceps, deltoids and trapezius.

LOWER-BACK EXERCISES

This is one part of a cyclist's body that fatigues easily if left untrained, especially early in the season or on long rides. While cyclists tend to be quite flexible in terms of trunk flexion (bending forward), they are notoriously poor at bending in the other direction (trunk extension). Training the lower-back muscles will help improve posture and will most likely help transfer more force to the pedals, especially during seated climbing.

Recommended exercises include:

* Back extension
* Low rowing (can be considered upper-body pulling)

[BACK EXTENSION]

Back extension

PREPARATION If needed, pad seat area with towels for added comfort and to level the seat. Place hips on padded area and hold your legs straight behind with a training partner securely holding your ankles.

DESCRIPTION With hands behind the head, slowly lower torso as low as possible (head touches floor) and return to the starting position (torso parallel to the floor). Do not rise above this position.

CYCLING APPLICATION Torso position, climbing while seated, posture, stability while sprinting and pedal stroke.

MUSCLES Spinal erectors (spinalis dorsi, longissimus dorsi and ilio costalis lumborum).

ABDOMINAL EXERCISES

The abdominal muscles constitute one of the weakest areas for cyclists (and most other people, too). Weak abs reduce the power you can transfer to the pedals in sprints, climbing and time trials, and can contribute to lower-back pain.

A glance at the average cyclist's posture on the bike reveals that the abdominal muscles are usually not getting much of a workout. A bit of strength training here can really pay off, particularly in climbing or sprinting out of the saddle.

Recommended exercises include:

• Pulley crunch.
• Side bends.

[PULLEY CRUNCH]

[SIDE BENDS]

Pulley crunch

PREPARATION Fit strap to high pulley and roll pads to bottom hole.

DESCRIPTION Sit with hips and back flat against pad. Hands are located at shoulder level. Bend at the waist and curl down and forward until elbows contact thighs.

CYCLING APPLICATION Trunk stabilization (especially on drops) and climbing.

MUSCLES Rectus abdominals.

Side bends

PREPARATION Fit foot brace and T-bar to low pulley. Use chain to adjust length.

DESCRIPTION Stand at 90 degrees to the machine, with foot closest to unit on foot brace. Start with your hand grasping the bar positioned at approximately knee height. Flex the opposite external oblique muscle to return torso to upright position.

[LEG PRESS]

Repeat for desired number of repetitions on one side and then change to opposite side and repeat.

CYCLING APPLICATION Out-of-saddle climbing/sprints.

MUSCLES Abdominal muscles (external and internal obliques).

LOWER-BODY EXERCISES

The lower body is where most cyclists tend to concentrate during strength training. In some instances, this can be a mistake — to become faster on your bike, you may need a stronger upper body.

Cyclists' legs tend to be above average in strength as a result of riding. The pedal stroke is mostly dependent on hip flexion and extension, along with knee flexion and extension. The calf, or lower leg, is not thought to contribute greatly to the pedal stroke, but some work should be directed here.

Recommended exercises include:

• Leg press.
• Leg extension.

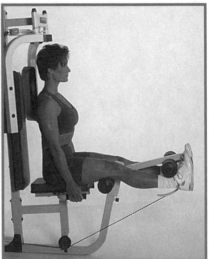

[LEG EXTENSION]

- Leg curl.
- Heel or calf raises.
- Hip flexion.
- Hip extension.

Leg press

PREPARATION Adjust lower seat so the hips are below the pressing platform. Adjust the seat back so the knees are comfortably bent.

DESCRIPTION Slowly push the platform away without locking knee. Keep feet flat against the platform while returning to start position. Leg press can be done with one or both legs.

CYCLING APPLICATION Pedal stroke.

MUSCLES Gluteals, quadriceps, hip extensors.

Leg extension

PREPARATION From a seated position, place feet behind lower set of roll pads. Grip the bottom of the seat.

[LEG CURL]

DESCRIPTION Keeping torso flat against back pad, slowly straighten knees and return to starting position.

CYCLING APPLICATION Prepares quadriceps for multi-joint exercises that assist your pedal stroke.

MUSCLES Quadriceps.

Leg curl

PREPARATION Facing the machine, hook leg around the lower roll pad. Grasp the top of the seat-back padding for balance.

DESCRIPTION Slowly bend knee to raise lower leg as high as possible. Return to starting position. After desired number of reps have been performed, rest a short time, then repeat exercise using opposite leg.

CYCLING APPLICATION Pedal stroke.

MUSCLES Hamstrings.

[HEEL OR CALF RAISES]

Heel or calf raises

PREPARATION Fit hip strap around waist. Fit waist belt to low pulley and adjust length.

DESCRIPTION Facing the machine, grasp machine and place toes on top of foot brace. Keeping legs straight, slowly rise up on toes. Slowly lower heels to floor.

CYCLING APPLICATION Pedal stroke.

MUSCLES Gastrocnemius and soleus.

Hip flexion

PREPARATION Fit ankle cuff to low pulley, then fit cuff around right ankle. Stand with legs straight.

DESCRIPTION Bend right hip and knee, bringing right knee as close as possible to chest. Slowly return to starting position. After performing the desired number of repetitions, place the ankle cuff on left ankle and repeat.

 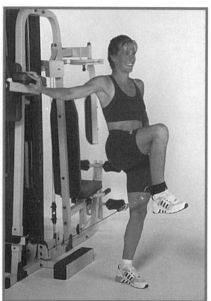

[HIP FLEXION]

CYCLING APPLICATION Pedal stroke.

MUSCLES Hip flexors (psoas minor, psoas major and illacus).

Hip extension

PREPARATION Fit ankle cuff to low pulley. Place cuff around right ankle.

DESCRIPTION Face the machine while holding onto the unit for balance. Keeping your knee straight, raise your right foot as high as possible behind your body in a kicking motion. Slowly return to the starting position. After performing the desired number of reps, place cuff on left ankle and repeat.

CYCLING APPLICATION Pedal stroke.

MUSCLES Gluteus maximus and hamstrings.

SUPPLEMENTAL OR SPECIALTY EXERCISES

Certain supplemental exercises are also available, although

[HIP EXTENSION]

they do not directly fit into any of the above five categories. These exercises may be used to add variety to the workout, or to address specific individual weaknesses.

Supplemental exercises include:

- Flys.
- Wrist curl.
- Reverse wrist curl.
- Shrugs.
- Hip adduction.
- Hip abduction.

Flys

PREPARATION Engage lock lever and move roll pads to top hole for leg room if required.

DESCRIPTION From the seated position, place elbows or upper arms against the bottom of the roll pads. Bring your elbows together so pads touch in front. Return slowly to the

[FLYS]

starting position. Maintain only a light grip with the hands, allowing the chest muscles to perform the work.

CYCLING APPLICATION Upper-body support while on handlebars and overall balance of body muscularity/strength.

MUSCLES Chest or pectorals.

Wrist curls

PREPARATION Fit T-bar to low pulley.

DESCRIPTION Sit on the seat and with palms up (supinated), rest forearms on roll pads, and grip the bar. Keeping elbows stationary, flex wrists until palms are above parallel to the ground. Slowly return to starting position.

CYCLING APPLICATION Aids in

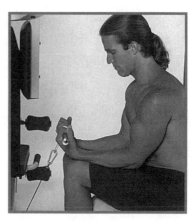

[WRIST CURLS]

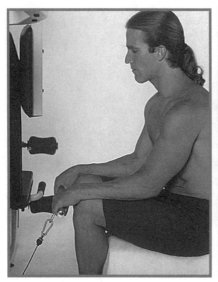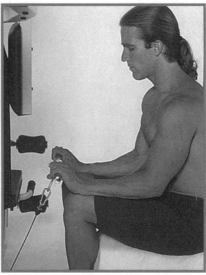

[REVERSE WRIST CURL]

overall gripping strength, which is particularly important for mountain-bike riding.

MUSCLES Forearm flexors.

Reverse wrist curl

PREPARATION Fit T-bar to low pulley.

DESCRIPTION Place hands with palms facing downward (pronated) and perform the exercise in the same manner as in the wrist curl, by lifting your hands above parallel to the floor. Return slowly to the starting position.

CYCLING APPLICATION Improves overall gripping strength, which is particularly important for mountain biking.

MUSCLES Forearm extensors.

Shrugs

PREPARATION Fit T-bar with chain to low pulley. Adjust the length.

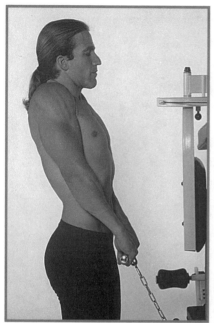 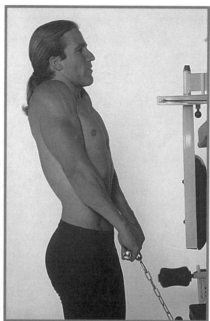

[SHRUGS]

DESCRIPTION Stand on and grasp the T-bar with palms down (pronated). Contract the trapezius muscles of the upper back in a shrugging motion. Slowly lower the lat bar. Shoulders should travel straight up and down.

CYCLING APPLICATION Reduces fatigue in the neck area, especially on long rides. Helps with out-of-saddle climbing.

MUSCLES Trapezius.

Hip adduction

PREPARATION Fit ankle cuff to low pulley, then fit the cuff around left ankle.

DESCRIPTION Face 90 degrees to the right from the machine. Keeping your left knee straight, bring your left foot across your right leg and raise it as high as possible. Lower to starting position. After the assigned number of reps are completed, switch

[HIP ADDUCTION]

[HIP ABDUCTION]

the cuff to the right ankle and repeat.

CYCLING APPLICATION Maintains supporting hip muscula-ture and contributes to stable and strong pedal stroke.

MUSCLES Tensor fasciae latae, gracilis and pectineus.

Hip abduction

PREPARATION Set up as for hip adduction, but place the ankle cuff on your right ankle.

DESCRIPTION Keeping your right knee straight, raise your right foot out to the side as far as possible. Slowly return to the starting position. After the assigned number of reps are com-pleted, switch the cuff to the left ankle and repeat.

CYCLING APPLICATION Maintains supporting hip muscula-ture and contributes to stable, strong pedal stroke.

MUSCLES Tensor fasciae latae, sartorius, gluteus medius and minimus.

TRAINING WITH FREE WEIGHTS

There are many cycling-specific exercises that can be per-formed with free weights or your own body weight. In this section, we'll only look at the basics. Most other movements are simply variations of these.

As with the weight-stack machine exercises above, you should divide your workout into six segments: upper-body pushing, upper-body pulling, lower back, abdominals, lower body and supplemental exercises. Starting with the lower body, exercises should include movements for the calves, quadriceps, hamstrings and hips.

Resistance training with free weights usually requires the use

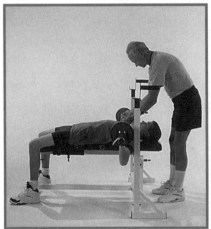

[BENCH PRESS]

of barbells and dumbbells. Both will be recommended for specific exercises.

Barbells allow the use of heavier weights in many exercises. However, if one arm is weaker than the other, this muscular imbalance may go untreated, since both hands are lifting the same object. And many exercises call for barbells to be placed on the shoulders or upper back, which can cause problems getting rid of the weight quickly and safely in case you lose your balance.

Since dumbbells are held singly in each hand, you won't use as much weight with them as you would with a barbell, though your arms and hands must constantly hold the weights, and can grow fatigued. However, if you need to drop the weights quickly for any reason, it is much easier and safer to do so with dumbbells.

If you are buying equipment, rather than using the free weights at a health club, you'll need a weight bench and a squat rack. Check the width and thickness of the weight-bench pad. Performing a bench press with a narrow, thin pad can lead

[SEATED PRESS]

to bruising around the shoulder blades and a general feeling of discomfort. And a squat rack's base needs to be wide enough to provide a secure resting spot for the barbell, even if you drop it heavily back into place.

UPPER-BODY-PUSHING EXERCISES

Recommended exercises include:
- Bench press.
- Seated press.
- Triceps press.
- Push-ups.
- Dips.

Bench press

PREPARATION Lie supine on a bench with weights safely located on uprights approximately at arms' length. Place head slightly in front of the weight, keep head, hips, and feet flat on their respective surfaces.

DESCRIPTION Lift weight off uprights. Slowly lower to a position on the chest about nipple level. Press upward by extending your elbows. Do not arch your lower back. Always use a spotter for this lift.

CYCLING APPLICATION Upper-body support while on handlebars; overall balance of body muscularity/strength.

MUSCLES deltoids, triceps, pectorals.

Seated press

PREPARATION Sit on end of bench or specially designed bench that supports the back.

DESCRIPTION From starting position with bar at the clavicles (barbell), or the shoulders (dumbbells), straighten elbows until arms are locked with weights overhead. Slowly return to starting position and repeat.

CYCLING APPLICATION Upper-body support while on handlebars; overall balance of body muscularity/strength.

MUSCLES Deltoids, triceps.

[TRICEPS PRESS]

Triceps press

PREPARATION Grasp a barbell or single dumbbell overhead (narrow grip), palms facing the ceiling.

DESCRIPTION Slowly lower the weight until the elbows are fully bent, then straighten the elbows to return weight to the overhead position. Do not let the weight bounce at the bottom of the movement.

CYCLING APPLICATION Support of upper body while on handlebar "drops."

MUSCLES Triceps.

Push-ups

PREPARATION Support body weight on hands and toes, body approximately parallel to floor.

DESCRIPTION Head up, bend elbows until chest touches floor. Straighten elbows to return to starting position, repeat. Keep torso rigid and straight. If too difficult, support body on hands and knees (feet elevated in the air). Perform the same movement with less-than-complete body weight.

CYCLING APPLICATION Upper body support while on handlebars, overall balance of body muscularity/strength.

MUSCLES Deltoids, pectorals, triceps.

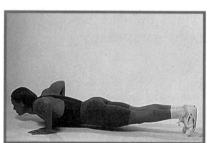

[PUSH-UPS]

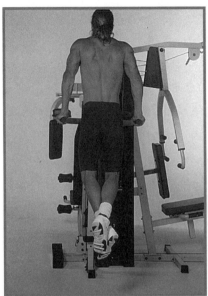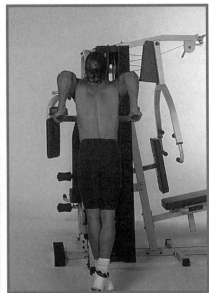

[Dips]

Dips

PREPARATION Fully support body weight from two solid and secure parallel surfaces, arms straight.

DESCRIPTION Bend elbows to slowly lower body until upper arms are approximately parallel to the floor. Straighten arms to return to starting position.

CYCLING APPLICATION Upper-body support while on handlebars, overall balance of body muscularity/strength.

MUSCLES Deltoids, triceps, pectorals.

UPPER-BODY-PULLING EXERCISES

Recommended exercises include:

• Dumbbell rowing.
• Arm curls.
• Upright row.

[DUMBBELL ROWING]

Dumbbell rowing

PREPARATION Support left knee and hand on a bench.

DESCRIPTION With right hand raise a dumbbell from its position on the floor. With arm fully extended, contract the muscles of the middle back, then bend the elbow to pull the weight up to the mid-torso level. Slowly return and repeat. Switch to the other side of the body and continue.

CYCLING APPLICATION Sprinting, hill climbing.

MUSCLES Latissimus dorsi, biceps, brachii, posterior deltoid.

Arm curls

PREPARATION Use a barbell or two dumbbells. Stand with weights hanging from straight arms, palms facing away from the body.

DESCRIPTION Using only the biceps muscles of the upper arm, bend the elbow until the weight is raised to chin level. Slowly lower weight to starting position and repeat.

CYCLING APPLICATION Sprinting, hill climbing, pulling on handlebars.

MUSCLES Biceps.

[ARM CURLS]

[UPRIGHT ROW]

Upright row

PREPARATION Stand with a barbell hanging in front of the thighs with arms straight. Grasp the barbell with hands four to six inches apart, palms facing the body.

DESCRIPTION Using the upper back and biceps muscles,

bend the elbows, raising the weight until it reaches nipple height. Raise elbows to approximately ear level.

CYCLING APPLICATION Sprinting, hill climbing, pulling on handlebars.

MUSCLES Biceps, deltoids, trapezius.

LOWER-BACK EXERCISES

Recommended exercises include:

- Stiff-legged deadlift.
- Good morning.
- Back extension.

Stiff-legged deadlift

PREPARATION Using bent legs and flat back, raise barbell from floor, leaving arms straight. This is the starting position.

DESCRIPTION Bend knees slightly, bend at waist while keeping back flat. Lower weight within a range of individual comfort. From lowest position, raise weight to starting position and repeat. If flexibility is good, stand on elevated

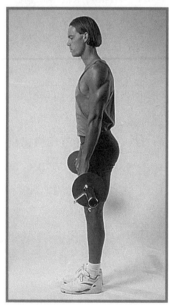

[STIFF-LEGGED DEADLIFT]

secure surface so weights may be lowered farther (bar is placed on top of feet at lowest position). This is an advanced exercise — caution should be exercised.

CYCLING APPLICATION Torso position, climbing while seated, posture, stability while sprinting, pedal stroke.

MUSCLES Spinal erectors, hamstrings, gluteals.

Good morning

PREPARATION Rest barbell on trapezius muscles of the upper back. Bend knees slightly and bend at the waist, keeping the back flat.

DESCRIPTION Bend forward to a position between 45 degrees and parallel to the floor. Return to starting position and repeat. Do not use heavy weights.

CYCLING APPLICATION Torso position, climbing while seated, posture, stability while sprinting, pedal stroke.

MUSCLES Spinal erectors, hamstrings, gluteals.

Back extension

PREPARATION Lie prone on mat, hands alongside hips.

[GOOD MORNING]

• Elevate upper torso off the floor by contracting the low back muscles. Return to the floor and repeat. For extra intensi-

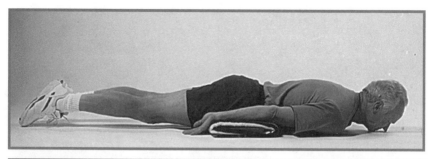

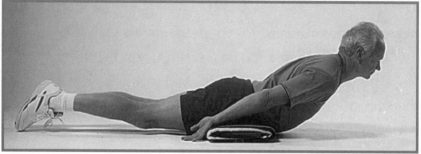

[BACK EXTENSION]

ty, place hands behind neck and execute the movement.

CYCLING APPLICATION Seated climbing, out-of-saddle climbing and sprinting, time trials.

MUSCLES Spinal erectors.

ABDOMINAL EXERCISES

Recommended exercises include:

• Crunch.

Crunch

PREPARATION Lie supine on floor with knees bent, feet either on the floor or supported on a bench or chair. Cup hands over ears or cross arms in front of torso.

DESCRIPTION Contract the abdominal muscles to raise torso until elbows touch knees. Return to starting position and

[CRUNCH]

repeat. Be sure to keep low back in contact with the floor. Do not yank on head or neck when rising from the floor.

CYCLING APPLICATION Trunk stabilization, especially on handlebar drops; climbing.

MUSCLES Abdominals.

LOWER-BODY EXERCISES

Recommended exercises include:

• Squat.

• Lunge.

• Heel raise

Squat

PREPARATION From a resting place atop squat racks, place barbell on trapezius muscles of the upper back. Stand up, step back two steps.

DESCRIPTION Slowly bend ankles, knees, and hips to lower body until thighs are parallel to floor. Do not lean forward excessively. Keep feet flat on floor. Straighten legs to return to starting position, repeat.

CYCLING APPLICATION Pedal stroke.

MUSCLES Hip extensors, quadriceps, gluteals, spinal erectors.

[SQUAT]

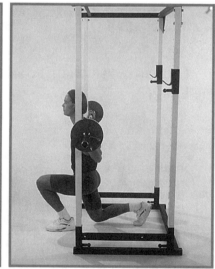

[LUNGE]

Lunge (free weights)

PREPARATION Place barbell on back as in squatting, or use dumbbells at arms' length by hips.

DESCRIPTION Step forward with left leg about 30 inches. Keep front foot flat on floor, rear foot balanced on toes, lower

[HEEL (CALF) RAISE]

front thigh until parallel to floor. Push back taking one or two recovery steps to starting position. Alternate legs.

CYCLING APPLICATION Pedal stroke.

MUSCLES Hip extensors, quadriceps.

Heel (calf) raise

PREPARATION Stand with toes of right foot on slightly elevated surface. Lift weight off of rack and rest on upper back.

DESCRIPTION Slowly rise on toes, then return to starting position with heels below level of toes.

CYCLING APPLICATION Pedal stroke.

MUSCLES Gastrocnemius.

Training tips

Here are some "tricks of the trade" to keep your strength-training program challenging and fun:

- Do multiple-joint movements first, saving single-joint

58

movements — especially for the arms — until the end of the workout. For example, bent-over rowing, which includes both the shoulder and elbow joints, should be done before arm curls, which only involves the elbow joint. Training small muscles and single joints first causes fatigue that can interfere with the proper performance of the more complicated multiple-joint movements in which you are lifting more weight.

• Only use multiple-joint movements during the Strength and Power phases. You will be handling heavier loads or performing quick movements, and doing these with only one joint could lead to injury.

• Change exercises about every four weeks. Even though you will have a favorite exercise in each category, it is essential to incorporate all the exercises into your training program.

• Change the order of your exercises. For example, don't always begin your training with the chest press — move it to the middle or end of your exercise regime from time to time.

• Regardless of which training phase you're in, your first set or two should be viewed as a warm-up, free of maximum effort. Be sure you add resistance after each set so the last set(s) will be difficult. If you are using lower reps (such as in a Strength phase), be sure the first set or two use higher reps (eight to 12) so that you get a proper warm-up.

• Reduce your training intensity every fourth to six week. Continue to perform the exercises, but use less weight. This "unloading" allows the body to recover and usually will result in improvement within a few weeks. When you return to increased intensity, begin with moderate weights that will let you use proper technique.

Injury-prevention tips

• Do not hold your breath during exertion. Slowly exhale during exertion, then inhale during recovery. Holding your breath can temporarily restrict your blood flow, resulting in higher blood pressure or blackouts.

• Always warm up before a workout. This warms the muscles and raises your respiration and heart rate. Jogging in place, jumping jacks, skipping rope or cycling on a stationary bike for a few minutes are excellent warm-ups.

• Always cool down after a workout. Ride a bike or take a brisk walk. Include some stretching, which will be discussed in the last chapter.

• Work through a full range of motion. This means opening the affected joints completely and closing them completely. Performing an exercise through a limited range of motion may lead to injury and a lack of flexibility.

• Weight-lifting belts are optional. A belt is generally overrated and does not reduce the likelihood of injury. If a belt is used, keep it snug during the lifting and loosen it between sets.

• Using gloves may help reduce skin damage, such as calluses on the hands. Cycling gloves work very well.

• Always perform your first set with a resistance which you can easily complete, usually about 50-60 percent of your maximum for the number of reps in your last set(s).

• Dressing warmly will help prevent injuries, especially during the cold months.

Safety tips

• Check your equipment (cables, pulleys, collars, pins) for

wear and tear.

• Never place your hands on the pulley system or reach under the lifted plate that supplies resistance. Make sure that the selector knob which sets the amount of weight is fully inserted. Check the lever that locks the bench arm and brings the butterfly into action when in use.

• Don't try to lift too much weight.

• Don't drop the weight stack at the end of a repetition; lower it gently to the rubber bumper.

• Place your hands or feet on the machine with care, so they will not slip off the roll pads or bars.

• If possible, do your strength training with another person for spotting purposes, especially if you use free weights.

PLYOMETRICS FOR POWER: START SLOWLY, THEN BUILD

As with weight training, your plyometrics program should include a well-defined progression in intensity. It is of paramount importance to emphasize coordination, fluid movement patterns, and correct motor patterns. Don't rush; make sure that you master each step before proceeding.

Following is a sequential program suggested for those new to plyometrics. The first three steps should be accomplished within your first few training sessions:

EXERCISES FOR NEWCOMERS

PROPER LANDING This exercise teaches proper foot strike; coordination of the ankle, knee and hips to absorb shock; and correct body alignment.

Begin with a standing long jump, with a two-foot landing.

This should be a submaximal jump with an emphasis on "sticking" the landing. Land quietly on the full foot; absorb shock by bending at the ankle, knee and hip. Repeat the exercise several times until you are comfortable. Next, hop on one foot, with the same objective as above. Repeat until comfortable.

STABILIZE YOUR LANDING This reinforces the correct landing technique and raises levels of eccentric and stabilization strength. This exercise is very similar to the landing exercises; the main difference is that you will hold the landing position for a five-count before initiating another jump or hop. Repeat until you can stick and hold three jumps, then three hops on each leg for a five count.

JUMPING UP This teaches the takeoff action and the use of the arms. Start with a stable bench or box at knee height. Jump up, onto the bench. Emphasize a forceful swing of the arms to transfer momentum to the whole body. Gradually raise the bench or box to mid-thigh.

BOUNCING This exercise will help you learn quick reaction off the ground and vertical displacement of the center of gravity. Before bouncing, review the first three steps outlined above; this will serve as a good warm-up.

Bouncing entails learning an ankle-bounce movement, which is essentially like jumping rope without the rope. Then complete a tuck jump, emphasizing quick reaction off the ground while bringing the knees to the chest.

With both exercises, you must keep the torso erect. Also check to see if your balance and body control enable you to stay in one place — if you cannot, then you should not move on. All of the above should be accomplished within one or two sessions.

SINGLE-LEG HOPS This exercise teaches horizontal displacement of the center of gravity. Begin by reviewing the previous four jumps. Then, start with three consecutive, repetitive, standing long jumps (two-foot takeoff and landing). Progress to five repetitive standing long jumps. Do the same exercise going up stairs, jumping onto every other stair.

Next, learn to single-leg hop and work up to 10 consecutive hops on each leg. Emphasize the cyclic action of both the hopping and the free leg; the action should resemble a single-leg run. Repeat this step for two to three workouts before progressing to the next step.

COMBINATION JUMPS This exercise adds more horizontal velocity. In this step, alternate leg bounding and various combinations of hops and bounds carried out for 10 to 20 contacts.

This is as far as you should progress in the first year of training. It is possible to increase the volume, intensity and complexity of the workouts by adding exercises and combinations of these first six steps.

ADVANCED PLYOMETRICS

DEPTH JUMPS This exercise, which raises explosive power to the highest levels, is an advanced form of training that requires a large training base. It is inappropriate for beginners.

Depth jumps consist of jumps off of boxes or rebound jumps over hurdles that are mid-thigh or higher. The training stress is high; therefore this method should be used judiciously.

Training tips
- At the beginning stages, double-leg takeoffs are preferable

63

to single-leg takeoffs. As your level of mastery of the exercises increases, the amplitude of the movements you make should also increase.

• Like other types of exercises, plyometrics can lead to poor results if not performed properly. Symptoms of tendinitis and synovitis, particularly of the knee, can result from too much plyometric training.

The frequency and duration of your plyometric training sessions should be determined by your fitness, experience and conditioning. Stronger cyclists can train more often and include more jumps. But not even the most experienced plyometrician should do more than two sessions per week, with a maximum of 60 to 80 jumps per session.

• You should have a sound conditioning base and have incorporated stretching into your program before engaging in plyometrics.

• Always conduct plyometric sessions on a surface that absorbs shock. Never do these exercises on hard surfaces such as concrete.

For more information on Plyometrics, see Don Chu's book, *Jumping Into Plyometrics.*

EXAMPLE OF A PLYOMETRIC WORKOUT FOR CYCLISTS*

L =Left leg; **R**=Right leg; **BL**=Both legs

1. Warm-up with broad jump, bouncing, single-leg hops.
2. 10-yard run to low boxes, start with right leg and hop with right leg to top of box, then alternate to left leg. Repeat exercise starting exercise with opposite leg. (Low boxes are about

16 to 18 inches tall, depth jump boxes are 24 to 36 inches tall.)

```
    R       L       R
R [ ] R   L [ ] L   R [ ] R
```

3. 10-yard run to low boxes, begin exercise by hopping with right leg to top of box. Repeat exercise starting with left leg.

```
    R       L       R
R [ ] R   R [ ] R   R [ ] R
```

4. 10-yard run to low boxes, hop over the boxes using the right leg for take-off and landing. Repeat exercise using the left leg.

```
R [ ]  R [ ]  R [ ]  R
```

5. Begin exercise by hopping off box with right leg and alternate hopping over and hopping onto boxes. Repeat exercise with left leg.

```
    R           R
[ ] R   [ ] R   [ ] R   [ ] R
```

6. Hop with one leg over to 24- to 36-inch boxes, then use other leg.

```
    R   L   R   L
R [ ] L [ ] R [ ] L [ ]
```

7. Use only one leg for a complete cycle, then repeat with other leg.

```
    R   R   R
[ ] R [ ] R [ ]
```

8. Depth jumps, using both legs.

```
BL   BL              BL
[ ] BL [ ] BL [ ]   or   [ ] BL [ ] BL
```

65

SUMMARY

You now have the information you need to begin your strength, power and plyometrics training. Select a weight you can comfortably lift for the prescribed number of repetitions. Perform the first set of each exercise with a resistance that is 50 to 60 percent of what you expect to lift on your last set. Add weight on the succeeding sets. Keep good records of the amount of weight you lift. Try periodically to increase the amount of weight you use on your last set or two. Gradually build up the number of jumps and the intensity of your plyometric program.

Your health is the No. 1 priority, so be careful with your lifting and plyometric techniques and the equipment you use. Strength training can improve your cycling performance, but you still need to convert this strength to on-bike performance.

CHAPTER FOUR

Developing a
Powerful *torso*

"By mid-March you should be living in the big chain ring."
—John Cobb,
U.S. Regional Cycling Coach

The importance of a strong torso in cycling may not seem obvious — don't your legs do most of the work? But the torso serves a variety of functions, including helping maintain good upper-body position, both in and out of the saddle; absorbing shocks; and bracing the arms and shoulders as they pull against the handlebars.

On the bike, your torso generally remains flexed, regardless of whether you are climbing, riding on level terrain, or descending. However, when you stand on your pedals, your trunk position changes significantly, becoming more upright. And even then, it remains somewhat flexed.

The muscles of the lower back are the primary muscles of the torso that are used during cycling. You may be already be including some back-strengthening exercises in your off-season program. However, training the abdominal muscles is also valuable, particularly for the prevention of lower-back problems. Both the back muscles and the abdominals work to stabilize the position of the pelvis, which is critical to the health of your lower back.

"If you don't work on opposing muscle groups, you're bound to have problems down the road," says Harvey Newton, executive director of the National Strength and Conditioning Association and an avid cyclist.

"Weak abdominals set you up for imbalances in strength and flexibility, which can lead to poor form on the bike. You may also tire more quickly during long rides."

The exercises that we will examine are designed to work the major muscles that you need to build a strong torso for cycling, including:

• The latissimi dorsi (lats), which start at your waist level and go up each side of your back.

• The lower and upper abdominals (abs), which run from your hips to the chest region.

• The spinal erectors, which extend the length of your back along the spine.

• The external obliques, which run from the lower rib cage and run around the midsection to the front of the pelvis.

Strength-training programs for the torso should focus on developing muscle strength and endurance. This means placing less emphasis on high-velocity movements and more on repeated, endurance types of movements, by doing more repetitions in each set of exercises. The following exercises require less than 15 minutes per session, three times per week.

BACK-STRENGTHENING EXERCISES

BACK EXTENSION Lie on your stomach with your arms extended over your head. Try to lift your arms and legs by arching your back. Hold this position for three seconds, then lower your arms and legs. Gradually increase the duration and number of repetitions. This exercise also can be done on a back-extension machine.

SEATED CABLE ROW Rest your feet against a foot brace, with your legs slightly bent. Grasp the handle or bar with an overhand grip, with your hands about as far apart as they would be on your handlebars. Start with your torso leaning slightly forward. Begin moving the torso to a position perpendicular to the floor, keeping the arms straight. Finish the movement by bending the elbows and pulling the bar to the abdomen.

LAT PULLDOWN While seated or kneeling in front of a weight-stack machine, grasp the bar with an overhand grip, about shoulder width or slightly wider. Be sure your arms are stretched fully overhead. Pull the bar down until the bar touches the upper back. Slowly return to the starting position.

Here's a simple workout that only requires three exercises, along with sets and reps.

Exercise	Body part	Sets	Reps
Lat pulldown	Upper lats	3	12
Seated cable row	Lower lats	3	12
Back extension	Spinal erectors	3	12

AB-STRENGTHENING EXERCISES

STOMACH CRUNCH OR BENT-KNEE SIT-UP This traditional sit-up, done on the floor or on a weight bench, works the upper abdominals. Initially, the weight of your arms and upper trunk may provide enough resistance; as you get stronger, you can increase resistance by holding a weight behind your head.

LEG RAISES This exercise is performed while lying on the floor on your back. Place your hands under your buttocks, with palms down; keep your elbows out so the small of your back is pressed against the floor. Your head should be up, with chin to chest, and your shoulder blades off the floor. Extend your legs straight out, with knees unlocked, and your heels resting on the floor. Use the muscles of your lower abs to raise your legs until they are perpendicular to your body. Then lower the legs in a controlled motion.

TWISTING CRUNCH This exercise works the external obliques, which take up more area than the abdominals; the obliques are a very important mid-section muscle group for stabilizing your trunk while cycling.

To work these muscles completely while working on the floor or a bench, instead of curling your torso straight down, you should do a twisting movement. Pull forward and diagonally with your right shoulder until it is directly over your groin. Focus on trying to crunch the right side of your rib cage down to your navel. Release back to the floor or bench and repeat with your left side.

Here's a 10-minute ab workout that you can couple with your back routine.

Exercise	Body part	Sets	Reps
Crunch	Upper lats	3	25
Leg raise	Lower lats	3	25
Twisting crunch	Obliques	3	25

SUMMARY

Cycling does little to strengthen the back and abdominal muscles. If they become weak, you will be more susceptible to back trouble. Research supports the notion that increasing the strength and muscular endurance of the torso can improve cycling performance and reduce lower-back problems.

CHAPTER FIVE

Indoor
cardiovascular
Conditioning

"At the age of seven, I spent every day training."
— Bjarne Riis,
Winner, 1996 Tour de France

As we learned in Chapter One, the principle of specificity dictates that you spend a large percentage of your overall training time riding your bike.

However, winter usually means that indoor training is the best option — and in some sections of the country, the only one — for maintaining your aerobic fitness.

Many home fitness stores offer several pieces of equipment, including indoor cycling trainers, stair-steppers, rowing machines, cross-country ski machines and slide boards, to keep you fit throughout the year.

Training tips

To get the maximum benefit out of every workout, you should begin with a short warm-up. Spinning in a small gear, walking on the stepper at a low to moderate resistance, rowing lightly for a few minutes — these are all good warm-ups that will gradually increase your heart rate and blood flow to the muscles. Include some stretching (see Chapter Eight: Stretching).

Once you have warmed up, start your workout, making sure that you stay within the "target zone" you have selected (See sidebar, "Finding your training zones," page 80). After your session, take a few minutes to cool down. This gives your heart and muscles a gradual chance to recover. Stretch after your exercise session to aid in recovery.

Chart 5.1 is an example of an exercise schedule for one week. It includes strength training and stretching.

ANAEROBIC ZONE

A higher level of training can help increase both your speed and tolerance for the buildup of lactic acid. This type of workout, done at high intensity — 85 to 100 percent of your maximum heart rate — usually consists of short, hard sprints or repeated hill running and is referred to as anaerobic training or interval training.

ROWING

If you are looking for an indoor aerobic workout to complement your weight training, a rowing machine can provide a tremendous challenge.

Why would a cyclist want to row? Rowing is a great all-around exercise: It strengthens the back, shoulders and arms as well as the buttocks, legs and abdomen. And, like cycling,

5.1 EXERCISE SCHEDULE

Day	Type	Workout
Monday	Strength; Aerobic	3 sets of 15 reps; 45 minutes on trainer; total 8 exercises
Notes: moderate day: 65-80% of max HR		
Tuesday	Aerobic	20 minutes on rower and 40 minutes on Spinning Bike
Notes: easy day; 50-65% of max HR		
Wednesday	Strength	3 sets of 15 reps total 8 exercises
Thursday	Aerobic & Anaerobic	50 minutes on trainer with 15/20/15 workout
Notes: hard day. 15 min: 60-85% max HR; 20 min: 4 intervals of 2 min hard and 3 min easy; 15 min: 60-85% max HR		
Friday	Strength	3 sets of 15 reps total 8 exercises
Notes: increase weight on chest press and hack squats		
Saturday	Day-off	
Sunday	Aerobic	20 minutes on rower and 1 hour on trainer
Notes: moderate day: 60-85% max HR		

it is a non-weight-bearing activity, which means you'll avoid the pounding that can be experienced during running.

Contrary to popular belief, rowing does not require arms like Popeye the Sailor Man. The rowing motion is initiated by a powerful leg drive, followed by the use of the back, arms and shoulders. The majority of power in the stroke comes

Training zones

FINDING YOUR TRAINING ZONE

As with strength training, in which different phases achieve different results, aerobic training has different training zones. Each has its own benefits and results.

The three primary training zones are:
- Fat-burning.
- Target heart rate.
- Anaerobic.

HEART-RATE TRAINING ZONES

Zone type	% of max HR
Fat Burning	50 to 65
Benefit Low level intensity — weight control	
Target HR	60 to 85
Benefit Builds aerobic endurance	
Anaerobic	85 to 100
Benefit Builds power — speed	

FAT-BURNING ZONE

This zone's level of intensity is moderate enough to require your body to use fat as its primary fuel source. You should exercise at 50 to 65 percent of your maximum heart rate to achieve this level of intensity (multiply your max heart rate by 0.50 and 0.65 to determine your upper and lower limits for this zone).

TARGET HEART-RATE ZONE

The second zone is known as the "aerobic-exercise zone" or "target heart-rate zone." In this zone you should exercise at 60 to 85 percent of your max heart rate.

Training in this zone helps you build aerobic endurance and constructs a base upon which you can progressively add more demanding workouts as your cardiovascular fitness increases.

from the legs.

Most machines that replicate the actual motion of rowing have the "oar" attached to a small handle that connects by a cable or chain to a flywheel that provides resistance while rowing. The rower has foot pedals and a padded seat that rides on the center rail. Resistance is changed by increasing the stroke rate. An electronic monitor will give you information on number of strokes completed, estimate of calories burned and time of exercise.

If the rower has a stroke counter, count the number of strokes you make during a particular interval or workout. You can also use the stroke counter to give you an idea of your rate of strokes per minute. This is similar to cadence while cycling.

Getting started with your rowing program should be handled like any other aerobic exercise. Always incorporate warm-ups and cool-downs into your workout, and do some stretching before and after you use the machine.

One word of caution: Lower-back problems can develop in inexperienced rowers. A painful lower back is usually the result of setting the tension too high and using poor form. Once you have learned the technique, you can slowly increase the resistance.

THE STROKE

One common mistake is to try to pull up and back with the shoulders at the start of the stroke. Keep your shoulders even and level throughout the motion. "Shooting your tail," or allowing the seat to fly backward under the force of your leg push while simultaneously leaning forward, wastes a great deal of power and stresses your lower back.

There are three parts to the basic stroke:

1) With your upper body leaning slightly forward, move forward on the seat, drawing your knees up to your chest. Your head should be up, arms straight and your back firm.

2) Push back on the foot pedals, exhaling as you pull.

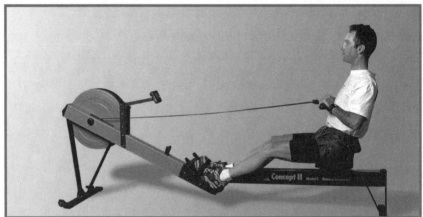

[THE STROKE]

When your legs are fully extended, continue the stroke by leaning slightly backward, drawing the "oars" to your abdomen or lower chest.

3) Come forward by rolling the palms of your hands downward on the "oar" grips. Then push forward with your palms and wrists. This movement works the muscles in your forearms.

Workouts

Generally, cyclists don't do a great deal of rowing in their daily lives, so it is extremely important to start gradually. Keep the resistance setting low at first. Beginners might start with sessions of 10 to 15 minutes, alternating two minutes of rowing with 30 seconds of rest, or aim for about 12 strokes per minute. As you get stronger, increase the duration and resistance gradually, with the goal of 20 to 25 strokes per minute.

When the rowing action starts to feel routine, you can vary the routine by adding sprints and intervals to your program. During sprints and interval training, you will be stressing your anaerobic energy system. Varying your training schedule is essential and will improve your overall performance on the rower.

Here are some ways to add power to your workouts:

• Try increasing the stroke rate for 10 strokes once every two to three minutes.

• Alternate three five- to six-minute periods of harder rowing with three three-minute periods of easy rowing. More advanced rowers can increase the time and intensity of their workouts.

• Alternate one minute of hard sprinting and one minute of easy rowing for a total of 20 minutes.

• Lengthen the periods of rest and make the sprints more intense: say, 90 seconds to two minutes all-out, followed by three minutes of easy rowing.

• If your desire is to lose weight, row at an easy to moderate intensity for longer periods of time.

• Design workouts similar to those listed in Chapter Six: Spinning Your Wheels Indoors.

Injury-prevention tips

Follow these guidelines to prevent injury on the rowing machine:

• Use your legs, arms and shoulders to do the work; avoid straining your back.

• Don't start the backward motion with your back. Start with your legs, then gradually use your back, using your extending legs for leverage.

• Make sure your shoulders stay even and level; don't twist your torso.

• Concentrate on smooth, economical motion that engages the muscles without undue stress or strain.

• Position your exercise equipment in the coolest part of your house. A room that is comfortable for lounging may seem like a sauna while you are rowing. A temperature in the low 60s is best.

STAIR-STEPPING

Although many people complain about climbing stairs, some cyclists have begun to brag about it. Many fitness researchers are discovering that stair-climbing is an excellent aerobic conditioner that provides conditioning for a variety of muscles used in cycling. Plus, it is an activity that many of us do every day.

Stair-stepping is great exercise for the buttocks, hamstrings and quadriceps — the key cycling muscles. When you add arm exercise to the climbing motion, you have a total-body conditioner.

[CYCLIST USING STAIRCLIMBER]

Stair-steppers use adjustable hydraulic cylinders, wind or electromagnetic brakes that give you a smooth and reliable stepping motion. Depending upon the model you are using, an integrated computer/monitor will provide readouts of time, distance, step count, pulse rate and calories burned.

The step

Whatever type of stair-stepper you are using, follow these suggestions on stepping correctly:

• Lean your body slightly forward, as if you were walking up a staircase.

• Look straight ahead, into a mirror if possible. This will help you maintain good form throughout the workout.

• Place your feet on the pads about hip-width apart. Your hips should not swing excessively.

• Begin with short strides. If you go into long strides immediately, you may pull a groin muscle or strain your lower back.

• On most models, use the handrails for balance only. To get the maximum benefit, your legs should bear your weight.

• Make sure your knees move forward, keeping your weight over your toes. If you place your foot in front of your knee and then try to lift up on that foot, you may strain your knee.

Targeting specific muscles

Altering the way you step will work different muscles.

• Buttocks: Take higher and deeper steps. You can work the buttocks and hamstrings by placing more weight over your heels (stepping flat-footed).

• Abdominals: Take shorter steps, keeping your feet a little forward of your upper body.

• Quadriceps and calves: Step more on your toes.

• Quadriceps, calves, buttocks and hamstrings: Mix quick, short steps with full steps. Short steps work the quads and calves; longer, full steps affect buttocks and hamstrings.

Some models of stair-steppers include arm levers that let you work your upper body while stepping. This will give you a total body workout similar to rowing or cross-country skiing.

The high-low workout

This endurance workout will vary your stepping technique and emphasize different muscle groups.

• Warm up at an easy pace for five minutes.

• For five minutes, pick up your speed a bit and take slightly deeper steps.

• For five minutes, take still deeper steps (this works the buttocks even more).

• For the next five minutes, step with your toes to work the calf muscles and quadriceps.

• For three to five minutes, go all out, increasing your stepping rate and resistance setting.

• Recover for three to five minutes at a slow to moderate rate and reduce the resistance.

• For five minutes, take deep steps with your weight forward on the toes.

• Cool down for five minutes at an easier resistance.

Other workouts

• To improve your ability to ride your bike out of the saddle or to replicate mountain biking, train each leg independently. Working at a moderate pace on the stair climber, press harder with the right leg for 25 to 30 repetitions, while pressing lightly with the left leg. Next focus on the other side.

• How often have you felt out of balance while trying to apply pressure to the pedals while on a mountain bike? To improve your balance, play catch with someone while stepping on the stepper. This can be accomplished by not holding on to the handrails and then having a partner toss a softball to you while you are stepping. This will work on your balance while you are trying to maintain contact with the steps.

• Walk backwards on the stair climber. This will help you work on your balance and step with your whole foot (flat footed) and will work the buttock muscles, which are the power muscles of cycling.

• To train your anaerobic energy system, work at a medium pace. Manually increase to a high level of intensity for 30 to 60 seconds, then return to a moderate level.

To design additional workouts, follow the suggestions given in Chapter Six: Spinning Your Wheels Indoors.

Injury-prevention tips

• Make sure the foot pads are not slippery.

• Beginners should start with short steps and advance gradually to longer steps. Be careful not to overstrain your groin muscle (upper, inner thigh) and lower back.

• Place the stair climber in the coolest part of the house. Temperatures in the low 60s are best.

CROSS-COUNTRY SKI MACHINES

Indoor cross-country ski machines seek to simulate the quality of cross-country skiing by imitating the sport's distinctive diagonal stride: The left arm moves forward as the left leg moves back, and vice versa.

Most cross-country ski machines have two sliding boards or foot pads that serve as your "skis." The "poles" are either a pair of handles attached to a rope-and-pulley system or a full-length lever arm, which may require both pushing and pulling. Some machines let you adjust lower- and upper-body resistance separately, to compensate for differences in strength. Expect to pay $450 to $1000 for a sturdy machine.

How good is the workout for the cyclist? Excellent. And that's not surprising, considering research has shown that cross-country skiers have the highest aerobic capacity of all endurance athletes.

For some, a ski-machine workout doesn't feel as hard as a stationary bicycle or stair climber, because the work load is divided among all the muscle groups of the body rather than just one group.

The NordicTrack Achiever retails for a little under $800. By using the calibrated resistance settings on the upper- and lower-body exercises, you can accurately measure, in pounds or kilograms, the resistance you're working your muscles against. The Achiever's adjustable legs let you elevate the machine to create a "hill" for still greater resistance.

Precor offers a machine made of aluminum, as opposed to NordicTrack's wood, and features a freewheel system, separate arm and leg adjustments, electronic monitors and elevated legs. It goes for $750 and is available in fitness retail stores.

All cross-country machines fall into main categories: independent-ski and dependent ski. When NordicTrack introduced the first modern indoor ski machine in 1975, it was an independent model. With these machines, the foot pads move independently of one another, giving resistance only in the kick, or push-back, phase. A flywheel and belt mechanism gives a smooth, continuous resistance, while a nylon cord-and-pulley system provides resistance to the upper body. They do an adequate job of simulating the kick-and-glide of outdoor skiing, but they can be difficult to master.

On dependent-type machines, the foot pads are linked by cables so that when one ski slides forward, the other automatically slides back, with resistance coming in both directions. While they can be mastered by even the most coordination-challenged exercisers, they neither provide the same overall workout as an independent machine nor come close to replicating skiing on snow. If you ski trails during the winter, the independent skier is the only way to go.

Workouts

Start gradually. Keep the resistance setting low at first. Beginners might start with sessions of 30 minutes or less that alternate three to five minutes of skiing with 30 seconds to one minute of rest.

As you grow stronger and more efficient, gradually increase the duration and resistance. Vary your routine by adding sprints and intervals. Here are a few suggestions that will add variety to your ski sessions:

• Try pulling harder for 20 arm swings once every two to three minutes.

• Alternate three- to six-minute periods of harder skiing with three, three-minute periods of easy skiing.

• Alternate one minute of hard sprinting and one minute of easy skiing for a total of 20 minutes.

• Lengthen the periods of rest and make the sprints more intense, say 60 seconds to two minutes all-out followed by three minutes of easy skiing.

BACK-COUNTRY SKIING

This workout simulates a short race or a hard workout out on back-country or tracked trails.

WARM-UP Five to 10 minutes easy; heart rate less than 60 percent of maximum.

STEADY-STATE WORKOUT 20 to 30 minutes; heart rate in the 70 to 80 percent range.

INTERVALS Increase tension on the skis and poles to simulate uphills. Alternate 30 seconds uphill, 30 seconds downhill (recovery), for a total of 20 to 30 minutes. Vary the times as your fitness improves. Elevate heart rate to 85 to 95 percent on the uphills.

COOL-DOWN Five to 10 minutes of easy skiing, or until heart rate falls below 60 percent of maximum.

Injury prevention

• Don't let either of your feet slide in front of the stomach pad. This puts undue pressure on your knees.

• Do lift your heel while your foot is going back, and always keep your knees bent slightly.

SLIDE BOARDS

I first observed the use of slide boards back in 1977, while working with Eric and Beth Heiden at the Olympic Training Center in Squaw Valley. Today, more athletes are using slide boards as cross-training tools for aerobic and anaerobic workouts.

In addition to conditioning the muscles of the legs, the demanding and twisting motions of slide-boarding will strengthen the lower back — helping stabilize you on the bicycle when pushing big gears or climbing — and the gluteal, quadriceps and hamstring muscles.

Slide training allows you to keep up your volume of training without any additional stress on your joints.

Slide training is a great cross-country activity that helps

Losing weight during the off-season

It's easy to gain weight during the off-season, when you're exercising less frequently and intensely. Monitoring the calories you expend during an aerobic workout can help you maintain your proper weight while providing the motivation you need to keep exercising throughout the winter months.

Your daily caloric balance will determine whether you will gain, lose or maintain weight from day to day. Caloric balance refers to the difference between the calories you take in — the food you eat — and the calories you expend through work or exercise. One pound of fat is equal to 3500 kcal (or calories) of energy.

If you'd like to drop a few pounds during the off-season, you may find the following guidelines helpful:

• Ensure that you are consuming at least 1200 kcal per day while dieting. This is the minimum for everyday body maintenance and health functions. At this caloric intake level, most nutritionists recommend a vitamin and mineral pill as a supplement, especially for women.

• You should not lose more than two pounds per week on a diet. Therefore, you should not exceed a negative caloric balance of 500 to 1000 kcal per day. This will help you trim down gradually, without losing lean body weight (muscle).

• Your diet should be augmented with an exercise program that provides at least 300 kcal or more of activity per day and at least 1000 to 2000 kcal per week. This is best accomplished with low-intensity, long-duration "fat-burning" exercise at 50 to 65 percent of your maximum heart rate (see sidebar, "Finding your training zone" on page 76).

• Include behavior modification techniques to identify and eliminate self-defeating diet and eating habits.

• Finally, and most importantly, consult a physician or registered dietician before dieting.

supplement your in-line skating, speed skating and skate-skiing training during the off-season, and will help strengthen your leg and torso muscles.

The equipment

Most slide boards are two-piece units consisting of a polymer sliding sheet placed over a rubber base mat to keep the board from sliding out of position. The base mat also functions as a damper, reducing impact forces that occur when pushing off and stopping. Prices range from $80 to several hundred dollars.

Resistance is obtained when the thin gliding surface conforms to the compressible base mat; it can be varied by changing the firmness or thickness of the mat. This provides the feel of fast or slow ice or snow. Do not use a board on carpet — most are too soft and do not allow for proper gliding.

Slide boards come with permanent or movable bumpers at each end of the board, usually angled at 20 to 40 degrees. Avoid boards with hard vertical bumpers because of the potential for ankle and knee stress upon impact.

Board length varies from 6 to 12 feet. Boards with movable bumpers permit length adjustment for specific exercises, and allow you to lengthen the board as your technique and strength improve. Board width is also important — 30 inches is a minimum.

A pair of shoe covers is supplied with each slide board (you can also use clean socks). Shoe covers allow for smooth sliding, but make sure the covers and board stay clean. Periodically polish the board with inexpensive furniture polish.

The technique

Athletes who use the slide boards at the Olympic Training Center in Colorado Springs usually pick up the basic sliding movement very quickly. After a few practice sessions, you should be able to move laterally without hesitation.

When starting, keep your weight forward on the balls of both feet. Bend your knees about 50 to 75 degrees. Place the ball of your pushing foot on the bumper, and raise the heel of the gliding foot slightly, which will help transfer your weight to the pushing foot. Your back should be arched and your head up.

Push off with the foot against the bumper, and transfer about 60 percent of your weight to the gliding foot. Keep the gliding leg knee bent so that it stays positioned over your foot as you slide. Extend the pushing leg as you push off. Leave the pushing leg extended as you move across the plastic sheet. In effect, you are dragging the pushing leg while gliding.

As you move across the board, the gliding foot moves ahead of the knee. Stopping involves nothing more than flexing or bending the knee of the gliding leg when you contact the opposite bumper. Most of your weight should be on the ball of your foot as it contacts the bumper. When your feet are together on the bumper, repeat the initial movement to return to the other side. Push, glide, stop — that's all there is to the exercise.

Workouts

As with any training device, workout variety is important, and is only limited by your imagination. Monitor your heart rate (see sidebar, "Finding your training zone" on page 76) to determine the level of stress each workout places upon your cardiovascular system.

ENDURANCE TRAINING Begin gradually to develop your technique. Begin by gliding for up to two minutes, rest for one to two minutes, then repeat. Continue for 15 to 30 minutes. Gradually work on your endurance and back strength until you are able to glide 15 minutes without stopping.

SPRINT WORK Once you've become proficient at slide-boarding, see how many times you can make contact with bumpers in 15 or 20 seconds, with a 15- to 20-second rest. Build up to 10 sets. As you become stronger, increase the time interval to 30 seconds.

INCREASED RESISTANCE Harvey Newton, author of the video, "Weight Training for Cycling," has some advice for adding additional resistance to help strengthen the legs. Use a board about 6 feet long, and slip a half-inch-wide, 8-to 12-inch-long rubber band over your ankles. Slide back and forth for 20 to 30 slides. Rest for about one minute and repeat several times.

SUMMARY

Unlike cycling and running, a rower works all of your major muscle groups. While you simulate the motion of rowing a boat through water, your legs, upper body and midsection work together against the resistance.

Using a stationary rowing machine is also a great way to expend calories as you slide your way to fitness. Depending on your skill and workout intensity, you burn between 7 and 25 calories per minute — nearly as many as cross-country skiing, the other total-body exercise. Rowing also ranks closely to cross-country skiing in terms of aerobic conditioning.

Correct intensity is the key to proper form on stair-steppers. Too much resistance leads to the most common mistakes: supporting weight on the handrails and flexing forward at the waist. Locking your elbows to support your body weight means less work for your cardio-respiratory system. Use the handrails for balance only. Assume an upright, "neutral" stance with the shoulders, hips, knees and ankles aligned. The manual settings on the stair-steppers — unlike pre-programmed settings on other models — gives you complete control of intensity, which allows you to establish a base of cardiovascular fitness and learn proper form.

CHAPTER SIX

Spinning *your* Wheels Indoors

"Spinning will help the muscles develop elasticity. This is the quality which permits you to change the rhythm of your legs instantly, something that is essential for success in racing."
— *Francesco Moser,*
World champion on road and track

The biggest problems with winter cycling are early darkness and foul weather. For most of us who must juggle training with busy schedules, indoor cycling on a wind or magnetic trainer becomes the only real choice.

Some cyclists grumble that indoor cycling is a tedious alternative to "real" cycling. But the controlled environment of a trainer allows you to isolate and concentrate upon specific areas of your cycling fitness and technique.

For example, you can improve your ability to spin by simply listening to the trainer. If you hear a "whoosh-whoosh-whoosh" on the downstrokes, you are not pedaling properly. Concentrate on pedaling in circles — begin the power stroke earlier at the top, and pull your foot across the bottom of the stroke. After a while, you will develop a longer, smoother

[ROLLERS]

application of power throughout the entire pedal stroke.

With a little planning and analysis, you can ensure that every trainer session is a quality workout, making the most of your exercise time. And with a little imagination, you can keep the workouts entertaining ... even though the scenery never changes.

THE EQUIPMENT

Many bike shops offer both rollers and stationary trainers for indoor training. However, other, similar units can be used for the workout routines described.

Rollers

Rollers consist of three round cylinders mounted on bearings and fixed to a frame. A belt connects one of the rear cylinders to the front cylinder to keep the front wheel spinning at

[MAG TRAINER]

the same speed as the rear.

Rollers sharpen your bike-handling skills because you must rely on skillful steering and balance. They teach you to work on smooth, fast spinning, but offer very little resistance unless you add a fan or magnetic unit.

It may take some time for you to feel relaxed and confident on your rollers. However, once you're past the learning stages, the bike-handling skills you obtain will make you a more confident and successful cyclist.

Wind and magnetic trainers

Wind trainers have two fan units with slotted blades that churn the air. Magnetic trainers have powerful magnets and a non-conductive disk that produces resistance and dissipates energy as heat. Most of the mag trainers on the market have several resistance settings (low to high) and are controlled by a bar-mounted lever.

A wind trainer's greatest advantage for indoor training is that it increases resistance exponentially, closely mimicking the resistance that you experience on the road. If you were to increase your speed from 15 to 30 mph, you would need to increase your power output by a factor of about eight. The disadvantages of wind trainers are the noise generated by the fans and the lack of variable resistance.

With mag resistance units, resistance increases in direct proportion to speed, which is less realistic than with wind trainers. But they do provide enough drag to elevate your heart rate. Magnetic units incorporate a small, precisely weighted flywheel, which creates a slight "coasting" sensation and helps you pedal through the dead spots in your pedal stroke for a more realistic road feel.

Fluid trainers offer resistance with a wheel turning within an oil-filled cylinder. Advantages of mag and fluid trainers over the wind trainer include reduced noise levels and the ability to vary resistance.

MAKE THE INDOORS INTERESTING

Before you jump on the bike and start a long ride to nowhere, here are some tips for getting the most out of your indoor cycling sessions:

• Be creative. Make some training tapes that include your favorite songs (preferably something with a strong beat), and put on your headphones when you start to pedal. However, don't let your attention wander — steady pedaling in front of the television watching movie reruns or MTV is fine for the first few workouts, but it's a sure guarantee your mind will eventually mutiny, and your body will surely follow.

• Shun marathon sessions in favor of short, hard rides. Instead of two hours of spinning in a 42x18 while watching TV, do 45 minutes of intervals. The time will go much faster, and you'll get maximum results.

• Monitor your workouts with a bike computer, keeping a log of times, distances, and speeds, and use a heart-rate monitor to gauge the intensity of your effort.

• Don't overdo it. Chris Carmichael, USA Cycling's former national coaching director, recommends that you not spend more than two hours per day on the trainer. Chances are you won't be able to last that long — for most cyclists, 45 minutes is about the limit.

• Don't ride every day — every other day is plenty. Engage in other activities during your breaks from the indoor trainer — running, skiing and snowshoeing are all good alternatives.

• Finally, remember that when you ride indoors, there is no cooling airflow past your body. Use a fan to keep you cool — overheating will affect your performance and increase your heart rate — and fill your water bottle. Consider riding in the coolest part of the house; some cyclists set up their rollers in an unheated part of their homes, such as a garage or basement.

Workouts

Following are examples of several workouts that can be used on bicycle trainers. Variations of these workouts can also be used on stair-steppers and rowers.

Begin and end every session with at least five minutes of easy riding. If you cannot do all of the sets or complete the following exercises at first, just do whatever you can, and gradually work up to a session that lasts from 45 to 60 minutes.

Descending ladder

Start with a 10-minute hard effort followed by two minutes of easy spinning for recovery. The next set is eight minutes hard, two minutes easy. Each hard set decreases by two minutes, but increases slightly in intensity. The easy set remains the same. The workout ends when you reach two minutes hard and two minutes easy.

Pyramids

In pyramids, your exercise intervals increase in duration or intensity to a point, then decrease. For example, you could go one minute hard, one minute easy, two minutes hard, two minutes easy, three hard, three easy, four hard, four easy; then descend to three and three, two and two, and one and one. Or you could keep the time element constant and gradually increase the load. For example, pick a steady cadence and go to a smaller rear cog every two minutes until you reach your highest gear, at which point you lower your gear by one cog every two minutes. Beginners may want to use one-minute intervals instead of two minutes.

Surge and purge

Do this set three times through: Five minutes in a hard gear in your flat-terrain riding position, then three minutes in your seated-climbing position in an easier gear, but at a higher cadence, so that your speed stays nearly the same. Use the high-cadence session to flush the lactic acid from your muscles. Then return to your standard riding position and the hard gear for three minutes. Spin easy for three minutes to recover before the next set.

This exercise is good practice for recovering during a race, when you have to surge to drop someone, or if you have gone too hard and have to let your legs recover. Change your hand positions during these sets to break up the monotony.

Anaerobic threshold

This workout will help you build your sustainable pace, which will pay off during long races and climbs.

Complete 20 minutes (or 10 sets) of the following: One minute in a 42x15, cadence at about 110 rpm and heart rate at 65 to 80 percent of maximum; then one minute in a 53x15, cadence about 90, and heart rate at 75 to 90 percent of maximum. Build up to two, 20-minute sets or one, 30-minute set.

The gearing changes let you increase your heart rate without fatiguing your muscles. You should not feel a "burn" in your muscles if you are doing these intervals correctly; simply make your gear changes and concentrate on your cadence. As you improve, you can choose to increase the duration of the set or increase the resistance, or both.

Climbing

Use the trainer to simulate climbing. Select a gear that increases the load sufficiently to require a drop of 15 to 20 rpm from your normal cadence. Slide back in the saddle, and picture yourself on a long climb. Maintain this workload until hyperventilation or leg fatigue brings your rpm significantly lower. Shift to a lower gear and recover completely before attempting another bout at the higher resistance. This develops your leg strength and technique to push those bigger gears or struggle when the hill steepens.

Speed work

Complete five of the following efforts continuously for 10 minutes: One minute in 42x17 or 18 at 90 rpm (heart rate 90 to 95 percent of maximum); then one minute in 52 or 53x17 at 90 rpm (heart rate 75 to 90 percent of maximum). Your heart rate will climb steadily throughout the 10-minute set. Follow this with five minutes of recovery in a lower gear and lower cadence.

Next, do five of the following: 45 seconds in 52 or 53x17 at 90 rpm; 15 seconds, cadence 110-120 at 90 to 95 percent of maximum heart rate. Take one minute of active recovery between each sprint.

Finish with three 30-stroke sprints at 110 to 120 rpm. Make sure you have a good cool-down.

Intervals

Try one of the following workouts:

• Alternate 10 to 12 all-out, 15-second efforts with 45 seconds of easy pedaling.

• Three to six reps of three minutes at 90 rpm in a big gear, with three minutes of low-gear spinning between efforts.

Endurance

Begin cycling with low to moderate gears, and gradually raise your rpm or gearing until your heart rate reaches 75 percent of maximum. Keep it there for a half-hour; if your heart rate falls below or rises above this zone, increase or decrease your effort. Cool down for five to 10 minutes until your heart rate has dropped below 110-120 bpm.

One-legged cycling

Most of us are not symmetrical in our application of power to the pedals. Favoring one leg or the other results in asymmetrical pedaling and a reduction in pedaling power. Single-leg efforts can help correct this imbalance.

Place one foot on a 16-inch box. With the other leg, and in a low gear, try to pedal smooth circles for five to 10 minutes. Repeat with the other leg. This technique will improve your ability to apply power over a larger portion of the crank circle.

After several weeks of working both legs, slip the trainer into a very low gear. Using both legs, attempt to pedal with smooth power application. This is what professional cyclists refer to as pedaling with "suppleness."

Injury-prevention tips

• When you are first learning to ride rollers, mounting with the aid of a wall or chair will help you maintain your balance. Once aboard, the more momentum you can give your wheels, the more stable the bicycle will be.

• Whether you're riding the rollers or a wind trainer, strive to pedal smoothly, without bouncing. Concentrating on a

Stationary Training: The Arnie Baker Method

— by Arnie Baker —

Many people resort to riding stationary trainers only when the weather is cold or rainy, or when they are on a trip and restricted to a hotel gym.

But there is value in trainer workouts all year around — and some of the benefits of stationary cycling are hard to get in any other way. Stationary cycling provides a precise, cycling-specific workout that requires neither daylight nor pleasant weather — though you'll want to use a couple of large fans to keep you cool during your "rides."

And indoor training need not be a solitary experience. Consider forming a stationary-trainer group and "riding" together. Trainers allow faster riders to ride with slower ones — no one gets dropped, and everyone gets a good workout.

I've been running winter workouts for more than 10 years. I expect 150 riders a week to train with me on my patio in San Diego, where we could ride on the road if we wanted to.

WHICH TRAINER TO BUY?

Get a conventional trainer, one on which you mount your bike after taking off the front wheel, or a "track-stand" type trainer that cradles your rear wheel. Conventional trainers are more stable, but less portable.

Resistance should be supplied by fans. They're noisier than magnet- or fluid-resistance trainers, but they work better. In our experience, magnetic-resistance trainers perform imperfectly. The "magnet" seems lumpy. As effort and cadence increase, the magnetic resistance does not vary, so you don't get the right "road feel." Fluid-resistance trainers have a better road feel than mags, but I still prefer fan resistance.

WHICH BIKE TO USE?

Use an old bike. Enormous

pressures are generated on the bicycle when it doesn't move freely beneath you. The bike you use on the trainer will become wet with sweat, and rusted; the headset, with the bike always "going" straight ahead, will get grooved.

For these and many other good reasons, don't use an expensive bike on your stationary trainer. Any old or used bike will do — just make sure it is set up identically to your regular bike.

You might consider changing your cogset for indoor cycling, however. The setup that has worked best for most of my riders is a 12-13-14-15-16-17-20-28. The closely spaced high gears allow you to precisely tune the hard efforts. The large 28-cog allows you to work on spin and leg speed without muscle strength or aerobic capacity limiting the drill.

Finally, specific workout plans demand a cadence-equipped computer, which allows you to precisely tune your efforts, see your progress, and record your improvement. A heart rate-monitor also gives you important feedback about your workout.

PLANNING YOUR WORKOUTS

The secret of falling in love with stationary training is to have a plan, a goal. Many people find it hard to ride trainers for more than a half-hour. But they usually ride at the same speed and in the same gear. Challenging variation is required.

The chart below depicts a typical workout. Between each exercise is an easy-pedaling rest period. Gears and cadences are meant to be examples only. Fitness, trainer

Duration	Exercise	Gear	RPM	Intervals
10 minutes	Warm-up	39/21	to 120	
20 minutes	Isolated leg	53/17	50-60	4 & 3 min. reps
10 minutes	Hill climbing	53/14	50-60	
25 minutes	Progressive	53/16	80	2, 9-min. reps
20 minutes	30-sec intervals	53/16	100+	8, 30-second reps
10 minutes	Cool-down	39/21	100	

type, and trainer set-up all affect power output and make a predetermined gear selection impossible.

• Warm-up. Use the easiest gear available. Start at about 60 rpm — a cadence pedaling one stroke every second. Build up 5 rpm every minute until you are spinning about 120 rpm. If you are new to cycling, it may take some time to be able to spin this quickly.

• Isolated leg training. One of the best ways to work on leg strength is one leg at a time, resting the non-working leg on the back of the trainer, a box or chair.

Off-season is perhaps the best time to work on muscle strength. By pedaling with just one leg — isolating that leg — you can focus on pulling up, on evenly applying force to the pedals around the stroke, and on building tremendous push-down forces.

The key is to focus on the leg, not the cardiovascular system — which is precisely what it does. An easy gear will force you to concentrate on smoothness and the pulling-up motion of your leg.

A hard gear will, in addition, specifically strengthen your quads and glutes — the most important cycling propulsive muscles you have.

• Hill climbing. Place a 4-by-4-inch block of wood, perhaps 24 inches long, under the front of your trainer. Choose a very hard gear. Stand up and pedal 50-60 rpm. Build up to standing for 10 minutes. You'll feel more confident, and you'll be stronger at getting over real hills when you meet them.

• Progressive intervals. Here's a favorite. Choose a moderate gear, and pedal at an efficient 80 rpm for three minutes. Choose a gear that's hard enough so that at the end of these three minutes your heart rate is about 75 percent of your max, perhaps 140-150 beats per minute — too hard to comfortably carry on a conversation.

After three minutes, shift to the next harder gear, and keep riding at the same cadence. At the end of these three minutes you'll be working very hard.

One more three-minute

interval in yet another harder gear. At the end of this three-minute interval you should be gasping, and your legs should be heavy. Another minute or two of work, without recovery, should not be possible.

Recover three to five minutes and repeat this nine-minute exercise again.

• Spin intervals. Four people make this next exercise fun, although you can do it alone. For large groups, do it with the group divided into four sections. When you have a trainer class of 50 riders, and each section has a dozen riders, it's great fun!

In turn, each rider, or section, pedals as hard as possible in a moderately-hard gear at 100-140 rpm for 30 seconds. Everyone else pedals easily at the same time. When the 30 seconds are up, the next rider or section takes over. The 30-second intervals progress through the riders until, after a rest of 90 seconds, it's up to the initial rider or section to start pedaling hard again. Try for eight, 30-second intervals.

• Cool-down. Almost as important as the warm-up and the work itself is a proper cool-down. Spin your easy gear up to 100 rpm, hold it for four or five minutes, and gradually spin down.

The above information is derived from Arnie Baker's books, Smart Cycling *and* The Essential Cyclist. *Arnie is a U.S. Cycling Federation coach and conducts weekly stationary-training sessions at his home in San Diego, California.*

smooth, fluid pedal style will avoid stressing your knees.

• Keep small children away from moving parts, so fingers do not become caught in fan blades, rubber bands or spinning wheels.

THE SPINNING® PROGRAM

If you can't bear the thought of riding alone in your garage, think about joining a Spinning® class, in which an instructor

[SPINNING®]

leads a group of exercisers on stationary bicycles through a vigorous, 40-minute indoor workout.

The Spinning® program keeps your mind engaged while offering the variety of any challenging outdoor workout — an excellent indoor training program for competitive cyclists. Music synchronizes the group and sets the tone for a great workout.

"The Spinning® program is an aerobic and power workout combined into one that combines fast, smooth pedaling and out-of-the-saddle riding along with visualization techniques," says Johnny G, developer of the Spinning® workout program. Johnny may be known to many of you as a finisher — in under 10 days — of the 1989 Race Across America.

Competitive cyclists will appreciate the fit of the specially designed Johnny G Spinner bike by Schwinn. The saddle and handlebar can be adjusted up and down and fore and aft, allowing you to replicate your normal riding position.

The bike employs a fixed gear attached to a heavy flywheel, which encourages a smooth, powerful, round pedal stroke. Resistance, which is changed throughout the workout session to simulate intervals, hills and sprints, is adjusted with a knob mounted behind the stem.

"The essence of the Spinning® program is fluidity," says Johnny G. "A Spinning® workout is when you can revolve the pedals at a high speed while staying in the saddle or while standing. An efficient spin is achieved when your legs are pushing and pulling the pedals in a complete circular motion and the body is not hopping all around the bike."

Part yoga, part Tour de France

My introduction to the Spinning® program came at a Schwinn sales meeting in Vail, Colorado, with Johnny leading the session. First, we warmed up, at about 60 percent of my max heart rate. Then, the ride started, with Johnny instructing us to increase both the resistance and our rpm.

We pedaled out of the saddle, alternating our bodies from a rocking, side-to-side position to a crouched position with butts over the saddle. Next, we pedaled while sitting down, with increased resistance that mimicked climbing a hill at about 85 percent of max heart rate. Finally, we pedaled while "jumping" — four counts up, four counts down, and so on.

We never stopped pedaling throughout the 40-minute workout, and Johnny's direction helped us avoid the temptation to "zone out," as can happen during a solo trainer session. When finished, I was exhausted, but exhilarated.

And, after downloading my heart-rate monitor, I found my heart rate ranged from 65 to 93 percent of maximum during the workout — similar to what I would have experienced on the road.

A Spinning® class can be an excellent addition to your winter training program. Classes are available in many metropolitan areas; for more information on where classes are offered at health clubs, call 1/800-Schwinn.

SOLO SPINNING® WORKOUT

If you can't find a class in your area, Spinner® bikes can be purchased for home use. Johnny G. recommends the following type of program for use with a Spinner® bike or a standard wind trainer. Make a tape of five invigorating songs and you're ready to ride.

FIRST WORKOUT Ride at a steady pace that varies with the music and throw in a few jumps.

SECOND WORKOUT Repeat the first workout, this time adding more jumps, out-of-the-saddle "climbing," and sprinting segments.

THIRD WORKOUT Warm up, then gradually increase the tempo during the first song. Increase your heart rate to about 80 to 90 percent of max during the second and fourth songs, while adding a few jumps and climbing segments. Recover during the third song, and gradually lower your heart rate to about 65 percent during the fifth song.

FOURTH WORKOUT Gradually increase your heart rate during the first song, then do three songs hard, increasing the resistance with each song (80 to 95 percent of max heart rate). Begin your cool-down with the fifth song.

SUMMARY

Whether you live in frigid Vermont or rain-soaked Seattle, the best way to keep from losing your cycling edge during the cold winter months is with the snowbound cyclist's best friend — an indoor trainer. This ingenious device, which simulates in your home the same kind of resistance you normally encounter outdoors, not only gives you a great workout, but can also help maintain or even improve your cycling form until you hit the road again.

A good training program includes a healthy mix of workouts. Try the hard/easy approach, alternating days of steady-state riding with power or sprint sessions. If you feel tired on a day when you are scheduled for a hard interval session, relax and spin for 30 to 60 minutes. You'll still have plenty of time during the rest of the winter to catch up on your training.

Note: Spinner® and Spinning® are registered trademarks of Mad Dog Athletics, Inc.

CHAPTER SEVEN

*O*Cross-training and
utdoor activities

"Golf pros hit balls on the range, swimmers practice with paddles on the hands, and athletes in other sports do other things that improve performance by enhancing muscle memory. Too many cyclists just ride their bikes." — *Mike Kolin,*
Cycling coach, author of Cycling for Sport

It's possible to be a four-season cyclist, if you have the wherewithal to spend your winters in Australia or New Zealand. Most of us, though, eventually have to turn to other pursuits when the snow and shortened days of winter force us to finally hang up our bikes.

That's the bad news. The good news is that there are plenty of things to do when the cycling season's over, including running, hiking, cyclo-cross, cross-country and roller skiing, in-line skating and snowshoeing.

RUNNING

One popular winter exercise is running. Regardless of what some people believe, running is not detrimental to cyclists. In fact, several national-team riders use running as part of their off-season conditioning programs. Most of all it is the least expensive form of off-season aerobic conditioning and can be done any place and any time of the day.

If you decide to run, be sure to begin each session with a warm-up and finish with a cool-down. A 10-minute warm-up period should include slow running or jogging, push-ups and flexibility exercises. The cool-down should allow adequate time for various body functions to readjust to normal. The length of the cool-down depends on the difficulty of the exercise session and on the environmental conditions. It will normally last from five to 10 minutes and include such activities as jogging, walking, and stretching.

The key to a successful running program is to go at your own pace, using your heart rate as the indicator of stress, and to keep the intensity of your running sessions well within your limits.

If you have trouble running continuously at the beginning of the off-season for 30-60 minutes, try mixing in some walking. Alternate running periods of 300-500 meters with 50-meter walks. The walking segments are important because they represent a semi-recovery period. This way, you never reach the exhaustion point, and you're less likely to develop muscle soreness. Gradually cut back on the walking while increasing the amount of running. Once you're able to run for 10 minutes or cover a mile without stopping, you can eliminate the walking intervals entirely.

Even if you're a national-class cyclist, you'll discover that running uses different sets of muscles in different ways, so expect muscle soreness at first. This soreness shouldn't be so uncomfortable that you can't keep running. If it is, you're overdoing it, and you should reduce both distance and speed until the soreness subsides.

The biggest trick to running is avoiding injuries; when it comes to recreational injuries, runners often lead the pack. However, unless you trip or run into an obstacle (or an obstacle runs into you), acute injuries are rare. It's the chronic stress of overuse injuries that dog most cyclists. Yet, that is why running is a perfect cross-training activity. The other activities mentioned in this chapter give you time to retreat and recover.

Keep injuries to a minimum by wearing shoes specifically designed for running and by incorporating a stretching regimen into your routine. Stretching before and after every run will provide the most benefit, but if that's not possible, do at least one stretching session daily. There's no denying that running tightens the leg muscles, particularly the hamstrings. Regular stretching helps develop the necessary flexibility in your muscles, ligaments, and tendons to enable you to run comfortably and remain injury-free.

So, ignore cyclists who take a perverse pleasure in pointing out the hazards of running. There is no reason to be running scared. It's a great activity for the lower body.

HIKING

If you want to keep exercising outdoors in the winter, have access to challenging terrain and don't want to invest in a pair of cross-country skis or snowshoes, consider adding hiking to your program once or twice a week.

Hiking is one exercise that has practically no disadvantages. Hiking a few hours a day is comparable to a ride of several hours. The uphills provide the best aerobic exercise. Thigh muscles get an excellent workout, and if the pace is fast enough or enough altitude is gained, your cardiovascular system is adequately stressed. Take the downhills with caution, though, and keep the straining and holding back to a minimum. Be careful of foot placement and don't overextend your stride.

It's okay to hike alone if the territory is familiar, but if you're going into unknown areas or on an extended day trip, hike with a group for safety. Always take along a pack with food, water and extra clothes. For additional resistance, add some weight to the pack — this will make your legs work harder on the trails.

CYCLO-CROSS

Cyclo-cross is a great, cycling-specific alternative to indoor workouts, and one that will increase your strength, power and bike-handling abilities.

A precursor to mountain biking, cyclo-cross differs from its more popular offspring in a number of ways. A true 'cross bike employs the cantilever brakes and knobby tires of a mountain bike, but on a road-style frame with drop bars, reversed brake levers and 700c wheels. And about a third of the typical 'cross course is designed to be covered on foot at a dead run, carrying the bike over obstacles, up hills and through muddy, open fields.

The best thing about a cyclo-cross workout is that it's rarely dull. The wide variations in terrain and weather conditions will keep your brain occupied with searching out the best line and send your heart rate peaking and plummeting like a roller coaster. You'll go anaerobic for short stretches while powering over short, muddy rises or running uphill with the bike; get some lactate-threshold work on the flats; and recover on descents.

If you're not running already, begin with short runs at a moderate pace on level ground, preferably in woods or pastures, or in a city park. Gradually introduce interval-style efforts, including jumping rocks or logs and uphill sprints; cyclo-cross runs are short, sharp efforts, not long, steady jogs. Keep the sprints down to about 10 to 15 seconds at first, then build up to 30-60 seconds. Once you've got your running legs under you, try running with a bike on your shoulder.

You should practice your riding on a course that has all the ingredients of a cyclo-cross circuit — uphills, descents, hurdles and mud. A cyclo-crosser must train to handle a wide variety of conditions and situations with minimum effort and maximum fluidity. Sections that you can bull through on a fat-tired mountain bike will require more finesse on a 'cross bike.

Here are two tips for getting you through the rough patches:

KEEP YOUR MOMENTUM UP You must always be searching out the best line down the trail, when there is traction to be had, and then applying lots of pressure to the pedals, in a gear that's neither too high nor too low. You don't want to get bogged down in too big a gear or let your rear wheel spin because you are in too low a gear.

KEEP YOUR BODY AND PEDALING MOTIONS SMOOTH This also applies to mounting, dismounting, cornering, dodging obstacles and braking. Keep them all smooth and you will waste less energy, saving it for those spurts needed in extra-rough spots. You'll also stay in better balance, so you're ready for the unexpected.

If you're already running and riding during the off-season, consider adding a 60- to 90-minute cyclo-cross session on Wednesdays. Spend the first half-hour honing your technique on your practice circuit, then do a hard half-hour, building up over a few sessions to an hour.

Once you're comfortable with your fitness and ability, enter some races on the weekends. It's more fun than riding alone — cyclo-crossers are a friendly bunch — and it definitely beats the hell out of exercising indoors.

Technique

Three techniques are basic to successful cyclo-crossing: getting off the bike, running with the bike, and getting back on the bike. Patrick O'Grady, a cyclo-cross racer and promoter from Westcliffe, Colorado, has been doing all three for several years and offers the following suggestions. He also recommends the book *Cyclo-cross*, by Simon Burney, available from VeloPress. "My articles on cyclo-cross are a catechism at best," O'Grady says. "Burney's book is the bible."

Getting off the bike

DISMOUNTING FOR A RUN-UP Shift into the gear you'll need at the top as you approach the hill, hands on brake hoods or bar tops. Swing your right leg over the saddle; move your right hand to the top tube, just in front of the seatpost; then unclip your left foot — putting your weight through your right arm onto the top tube — and hit the ground on your right foot.

Once you're afoot and running, flip the bike onto your shoulder by the top tube or the down tube, depending upon your size and style. More on this later.

DISMOUNTING FOR A ROLL-UP On an almost-rideable hill, stay on the bike until you start to lose the momentum you'll need to hoist it on the fly. Swing your right leg over the saddle, pushing down on the left pedal, then unclip at the bottom of the stroke and jump off. Run a few steps with your hands on the brake levers or bar tops, then shoulder the bike and beat feet.

DISMOUNTING ON THE FLATS Many promoters use barricades to handicap mountain bikes on fast or technical descents; they also add difficulty to flat courses. Technique is at a premium during these high-speed dismounts; you can either gain ground, or lose skin.

Start off slowly, with your hands on the brake levers, then add speed. This is why 'cross racers reverse their brake levers — rear on the left, front on the right. It's soothing to be able to modulate your speed as you charge toward a 16-inch-high wooden barricade in a half-dismount, with your left hand on a brake hood and your right on the top tube.

As you approach, swing your right leg over the saddle, between the bike and your left leg, and slightly forward. Place your right hand on the top tube and lean back, with your weight through your right arm. Wait until the last possible second, then unclip your left foot and land on your right.

Lift the bike with your right hand; your left remains on the bars or brake hood to keep your wheels straight. Hurdle the barricade, set the bike gently on the ground, return your right hand to the bars and leap into the saddle.

If conditions are particularly heinous, or if you're nervous, you can unclip your left foot and approach a dismount with it simply resting on top of the pedal. But premature unclipulation risks sliding off the pedal on bumpy ground, or worse, clipping back in by accident — leaving you locked into one pedal as you barrel into a barrier at 20 mph. A well-drilled, last-minute release is far preferable. Keep your cleats and pedals well maintained, spraying them with cooking spray or aerosol lubricant on filthy days, and practice, practice, practice.

Running with the bike

Shoulder the bike for extended runs, particularly when the going gets muddy. Some 'crossers like to set the bike down between hurdles erected in series, running with hands on bars and top tube. But the repeated lifting can wear you out if you're the typical beanpole biker who shuns upper-body resistance work.

There are two ways to pick up the bike, and two ways to carry it (mountain bikers whose bikes' main triangles are cramped by sloping top tubes may have to try a third).

PICKING IT UP If you're tall, try grabbing the top tube and palming the bike, shot-put style, onto your shoulder. Snake your right arm around the head tube to grab the left brake hood. Vertically challenged? Try using the down tube to hoist the bike, then reach under it to the left drop. Mountain bikers may have to reach over the top tube to grasp the down tube, then carry the bike like a portfolio (try resting the saddle tip on your shoulder).

Keep your shoulder closer to the head tube than the seat tube for a comfortable, upright carrying position (a shoulder pad liberated from a woman's sweater or blazer helps, too). Lean forward into run-ups, taking short, quick steps; if you must run down a tricky slope, lean back a bit. You can open your stride somewhat for a flat run.

PUTTING IT DOWN Hold the bars with your left hand, then take the bike off your shoulder with your right hand on either the top tube or the down tube. The latter lets you sort of shrug the bike off and into your hand, and may feel more natural. But set it down gently; a bouncing bike is nothing you want to leap onto if you hope to reproduce.

GETTING BACK ON Put both hands on the bars (tops for the flats, drops for descents, brake hoods for everything else). Leap off your left foot, throwing your right leg over the saddle; land on your right thigh, then slide atop the saddle. You'll probably stutter-step for a while, but strive for the clean, one-step leap from left foot onto thigh — it's faster and safer.

Stab your right foot down for its pedal (a proper dismount should leave it near 12 o'clock). Clip in and stomp on it, then clip your left foot in as its pedal comes around.

Equipment

Specific 'cross bikes are available, both as framesets and complete bikes, in a broad range of prices from a wide variety of manufacturers. But if you've already got a garage full of bikes, you might consider modifying one of them instead of adding yet another. O'Grady, who has raced 'cross on doctored road bikes, mountain bikes and 'cross bikes, has some suggestions here, too.

"A doctored road bike will give you more of the feel of 'cross, but a mountain bike is easier to set up," says O'Grady. "However, since 'cross, for most of us, is a sideline — a way to stay fit and build strength for road or mountain biking — consider using whichever bike is your primary racing machine."

Converting a road bike

Your road frame will probably have more aggressive angles, less tire clearance and a lower bottom bracket than a 'cross frame, but it'll serve for starters. Get rid of the bottle cages — you're going to be shoving your shoulder through that main triangle for run-ups. Lose the frame pump and saddle bag, too.

Remove the pedals and replace them with whatever you're using on your mountain bike. Don't forget your off-road shoes.

Raise your stem a centimeter, lower your saddle by the same amount, and move your brake levers a tad farther up the bars for a more upright riding position. If your bar tape is one of those slippery brands, consider something with a little more grip to it.

At the other end of the bike, swap your straight-block for a 13-28 and your slicks for knobbies. Sewups are best, but clinchers will do, if you don't mind the occasional pinch flat (a spare wheelset for the pit is an excellent idea for such occasions). Vittoria Mastercross and Normal Cross are excellent all-conditions fronts, with a file tread pattern; Wolber 28 Cross Extra or Clement Grifo Neve are all-purpose rears, with an arrow-and-block tread. If you're going with clinchers, the Vredestein Campo (700x28 and 32) is the best around, while the Hutchinson Cross mimics the Wolber nicely. Ritchey's Speed-Max Cross is supposed to be an excellent tire, too.

Your 53/39 crankset will do as is; snug your front derailleur up to the big ring to keep your chain from bouncing off as you jounce across hill and dale. If you've got $25 to spend on a 48-tooth outer ring, and time to rearrange your front derailleur, replace that 53.

STI and Ergopower are the coming thing in 'cross, so if you're using either on the road, keep it for the dirt. Still shifting from the down tube, or worried about foul weather or crash damage? Invest $100 or so in the aero' brake levers and bar-end shifters of your choice. You'll save weight, and bar-ends are nearly indestructible. Grip Shift works, too.

However you decide to shift, consider rearranging your brake cables so that your rear brake is on the left; it's nice to be able to modulate your speed when you're rumbling up to a barrier in a half-dismount, with your left hand on the bars and your right on the top tube. Your road pads will probably suffice for dry conditions. And when the going gets gooey, the minimal tire clearance of a road frame is going to set you afoot in short order anyway.

Converting a mountain bike

Mountain bikes are indeed legal in American 'cross, and this may be the best way to get your feet muddy. A few aficionados may turn up their noses when they see you with your straight bars and fat tires ... but you'll spend less time and money getting a mountain bike 'cross-ready, which should lessen the sting somewhat.

Pull off your bottle cages, saddle bag and pump. Do the same with the bar ends, banned by U.S. Cycling Federation.

Finally, swap the fat rubber for something a little skinnier (26x1.5" or 26x1.7"), which will lower your rolling resistance while increasing your tire clearance.

CROSS-COUNTRY SKIING

If you live in the "snow belt," it is almost impossible to go for a long ride between November and April. Snow-packed roads and short days do not lend themselves to long hours in the saddle. But you can still supplement your training with cross-country skiing, a great alternative that is becoming popular with many cyclists.

John Tomac, Sara Ballantyne, Greg LeMond and Davis Phinney are among the many cyclists who have found cross-country skiing an excellent complement to their year-round cycling programs. Cross-country skiing doesn't just work the muscles of the lower body, it also exercises the upper body, arms and lower back — areas that are used on the mountain bike. In addition to building the upper body and leg-power, cross-country skiing is a great way for you to maintain a high level of aerobic conditioning.

Skate skiing versus diagonal stride

Virtually all cyclists and enthusiasts who like to ski fast use the skating technique rather than the traditional diagonal stride. As the name implies, skate skiing emulates the motion used for ice skating — you push off from the inside edges of your skis. Once you've learned the proper technique, you can travel at a rapid clip and get a great workout.

Mike Kloser, a former pro mountain-bike rider who lives in Vail, Colorado, says: "Besides being a great cardiovascular conditioner, the technique used in skate skiing works the power muscles of mountain biking — the quadriceps, gluteals and lower back. The power a cyclist gains from skate skiing carries over into steep climbs, chasing others down steep singletrack and sprinting."

Don't plan on using skiing as a complete replacement for your other conditioning routines — you still need to be on the bike and in the weight room.

Chris Carmichael, USA Cycling's former national coaching director, and Skip Hamilton, a masters cyclist from Aspen, Colorado, both suggest skiing twice a week, and spending the rest of your time on the bike, whether indoors or on the road. The skiing should include one endurance day and one anaerobic-threshold day, with your heart rate at anaerobic-threshold level or slightly higher for 30 to 90 minutes.

Novices will find that their arms get tired before anything else. But slow and persistent effort will build stamina and skill. Take lessons — you'll be amazed at the difference. Or, for a succinct overview of the basics, get hold of *The Simple Secrets of Skating* by Lee Borowski (4500 Cherokee Drive, Brookfield, WI 53045). Borowski works with a number of cyclists in the Midwest who are making the transition to skiing for winter cross-training, and I found his book and video to be excellent resources.

Roller skiing

If you want to get into skiing shape before winter arrives, or if snow is scarce in your part of the country, consider roller skiing. The fundamentals are basically the same as in snow skiing.

"Roller skis have been used by world-class cross-country skiers for many years," says Borowski. "They are an excellent training device — the closest thing to actual skiing."

Everyone, even accomplished skiers, feels awkward when they first start roller-skiing. However, with the proper selection of equipment and adequate preparation, the experience can be safe and a great way for cyclists to maintain a high level of aerobic conditioning.

I have tested several types of roller skiers and talked to several excellent skiers about the roller skis they use in training. Two brands of roller skis — V2 by Jenex Inc., and PRO-SKI — rise above the others for quality of equipment, ability to control speed and close simulation of snow skiing. In less than two years, they have become the most popular roller skis in North America.

If you decide you want to try roller skiing, I suggest you select one of V2's dual-purpose skis, model 910 or 920. The 910 is by far the slowest dual-technique (diagonal and skate) ski on the market. So if you want a ski for aerobic resistance training, live where there are no hills, or are extremely interested in safety, this ski is for you. The PRO-SKI Roadline dual-technique roller ski (for classic and skate training) has a speed similar to what you experience for classical skiing in the winter.

You may be wondering why I recommend slow roller skis. Many nordic skiers around the world have discovered that roller skiing is less demanding than real skiing, and that roller skis must be quite slow to equal the energy expenditure of snow skiing. The latest information from several national-team coaches of major ski powers indicates that their ski teams are now spending 70 to 80 percent of their roller-ski time on slower classical skis, and the remainder on faster skate skis.

If you are interested in a little more speed or plan on practicing your skating technique, then V2's Model 920 is best for you. My diagonal stride on a pair of V2-920's was more stable than I've experienced on any other roller ski.

If you are interested in training your skating technique only, then I suggest you purchase V2's 700 series skis and PRO-SKI Skating, which are slightly shorter and lighter and designed for skate skiing only.

For those wanting more security or who have to return down steep hills after a hill workout, V2 offers Speed Reducers and a Braking System new for this winter season. With the Speed Reducers applied, unless the hills are very steep, you can slowly negotiate the hill. To further reduce speed, or to stop, apply the new V2 Brake. If you want more resistance for training on the flats, shift the Speed Reducers to the desired resistance. These can be purchased separately from the roller ski systems. You no longer have to walk down all those hills you worked so hard to conquer.

Both skis are available at better cross-country ski stores and can also be ordered directly from the manufacturer. Models range in price from about $200 up to $300. For more information: For V2's contact Jenex Inc., P.O. Box 1219, Amherst, NH 03031; 603/672-2600. For PRO-SKI contact Nordic Equipment Inc., P.O. Box 997, Park City, UT 84060; 800/321-1671.

Safety tips

• Roller skiing can be dangerous — understand the limits of your ability and equipment. You may want to seek the advice of a qualified skier for tips on technique and equipment.

• Practice in parking lots, be aware of traffic hazards, and stay away from hills until you're comfortable with your technique and your ability to stop.

• Finally, wear protective gear — helmet, gloves and knee pads.

IN-LINE SKATING

Droves of athletes, from triathletes to cyclists, cross-train on in-line skates in the off-season because the motion works both the upper and lower body. Skating develops the quadriceps, gluteal muscles and hamstrings, providing an extra lower-body workout that cyclists need in the off-season.

Tom Schuler, manager of professional road and mountain bike teams, says members of both teams in-line skate because it works many of the same muscles as cycling, and skating uphill is a great strength workout.

So how good an exercise is in-line skating? In a study for skate manufacturer Rollerblade, Dr. Carl Foster, coordinator of sports science for the U. S. Speedskating Team, found that in-line skating at a steady, comfortable rate for 30 minutes produced a mean heart rate of 148 beats per minute and a caloric expenditure of 285 calories in 30 minutes or 9.5 calories per minute. During interval skating, the caloric expenditure was 450 in 30 minutes or 15 calories per minute.

Running and cycling at the same heart rates burned 350 and 360 calories, respectively. Burning 300 calories took 25 minutes for running, 24 for cycling, 32 for easy continuous in-line skating and 22 interval in-line skating.

In addition, skating places less stress on the musculoskeletal system than running and may reduce the risk of injury to hip, knee and foot joints. In-line skating also develops the hip and knee extensor (thigh) muscles better than running.

But before you start skating, there are several things to consider to ensure a safe and effective workout.

Equipment

Three main components determine performance of in-line skates: boots, wheels and bearings.

BOOTS In-line skates are made of molded plastic or polyurethane. High-end models feature ratchet-style buckles, similar to those found on ski boots and some cycling shoes, for better fit and power transfer from body to skate.

The fit of the boots is critical. Buy skates that fit fairly snugly. Your toes should just touch the end when you're standing up. Most in-line skates come in unisex sizes and run wider than most women are used to (though many skate manufacturers are offering models of skates specifically designed for women). Get fitted properly, and consider adding an insole to accommodate, for example, a narrow heel or flat feet.

WHEELS Today's urethane wheels range in height from 64mm to 82mm and in hardness (durometer) from a soft 75A to a hard 93A.

Bigger wheels are usually faster because they offer less rolling resistance; however, they take longer to get up to top speed. A good size for training is 70mm.

Which durometer you use depends upon the surface you'll be skating upon. Generally, a soft wheel is used on rough surfaces, while a harder wheel is used for a smoother surface. The softer 78A is ideal for making hard and fast turns, or negotiating traffic on roads or bike paths. The harder 85A is designed for going fast over good surfaces.

Whichever wheels you choose, they should be rotated every 60 to 80 miles to increase their life and handling. They should be switched from left to right skate, and from heel-to-toe to the interior positions.

BEARINGS Bearings are similarly designed for various levels of performance. High-precision bearings have the low rolling resistance a skate racer requires; the greater resistance offered by lower-grade bearings helps keep speed manageable for the recreational skater while increasing resistance for the athlete primarily interested in getting a good workout.

At least one company, V-2 (Jenex Inc.) makes a wheel whose bearings are specifically designed for just this purpose. V-2's Carbonic Wheels are loaded with a viscous synthetic fluid that keeps the wheels from spinning beyond a certain number of revolutions per second.

Since these bearings, in effect, provide the "braking" action, the wheels can be made out of harder, longer-wearing material, which also means they will wear longer and transfer less vibration. Replace one or all four wheels on your skates to dial in the resistance you desire.

Which combination of boot, wheels and bearings should you use? It will depend on the surface you skate on most often, your training objectives and your pocketbook. As with bicycles, consult with people who make skating their business. Visit your local skate shop for accurate advice and up-to-date information.

Safety tips

• When you buy your skates, pick up some protective gear, too. Sooner or later you will fall — and it will be on a hard surface. Most beginners throw out their hands to break the fall, and as a result, some may fracture one or both wrists. I recommend that you buy wrist guards before skating for the first time. Knee and elbow pads will help prevent abrasions. And, as in cycling, a helmet may also be prudent.

• Avoid traffic at first. Begin by starting on bike paths or mall parking lots. Practice stopping, since stopping and turning on a dime will be difficult at first.

• Try to skate on good pavement. The small wheels on your skates are much more vulnerable than your bike's wheels to pebbles and cracks in the road or sidewalk.

• Lastly, avoid hills until you feel safe while stopping and secure while turning back and forth across the fall line. After you've put in some miles, try skating hills with safe run-outs, good quality pavement and little traffic.

SNOWSHOES: SOLITUDE, ESCAPE AND HARD EXERCISE

You can bet that when the early fur trappers strapped on a pair of wooden snowshoes and hunted for food in the winter snows, they weren't concerned about improving their fitness. And when the Inuit traveled from winter camp to winter camp, it wasn't for the third leg of a winter triathlon.

But times have changed, and like cross-country skis and hiking boots, snowshoes have returned to popularity — not as a survival tool, but for the training benefits they provide.

"For cross-training in winter, snowshoeing is an excellent

alternative to running for those living in snowed-in regions," says masters cyclist and coach Skip Hamilton. "You use many of the same muscles as in off-road cycling; and it does not subject you to the injuries of running."

Best of all, snowshoes are simple to use. They don't require special skills, expensive lessons or groomed trails — if you can walk, you can snowshoe. All you need is warm clothing and the desire to get a great workout.

Equipment

Today's snowshoes run about 8 inches wide and 2 feet long, and can weigh less than two pounds. Made of lightweight, space-age metals or thermoplastics, coated nylon decking and synthetic webbing, they employ binding systems that can accommodate running shoes, hiking boots and cross-country-skiing boots. One or more claws on the bottom of each shoe gives traction for climbing, even on the steepest hills.

You can rent snowshoes from many outdoor shops and Nordic centers. Day rentals generally range from $10 to $20, plus a deposit. If you choose to buy, quality snowshoes are moderately expensive: from $160 for the training models to more than $200 for racing shoes.

Technique

If you have never snowshoed, first find a trail with packed snow, or loose snow that is only a few inches deep. Keep your strides compact; after a few outings, you will have developed a natural rhythm and will be able to cover terrain that is not accessible on skis.

Some snowshoers use poles when the snow is deep or the terrain is uneven. Poles may be a hindrance when running, but when making steep ascents, they may provide extra thrust. They also help build upper-body strength.

Novices are likely to feel a day of snowshoeing in their hip flexors, quadriceps and buttocks, especially on hilly terrain. But if walking isn't enough of a workout for you, try running in snowshoes. Compared to road running, running in snowshoes involves lower knee carriage, shorter strides and harder arm pumping. The lower body's range of motion is similar to that used in cycling. And running downhill is really fun. The snow gives you a smooth surface to run on, and if you fall — so what? Get up and keep going.

Snowshoe racers train with intervals, hill work and distance runs — the same tools you use in off-road training. "Interval workouts completed on uphill slopes simulate tough power workouts," says Andre Bozell, a winner of the Vail (Colorado) Mountain Man, and a rider coach at the Carpenter-Phinney training camps.

Workout

Here's a good, simple snowshoe workout suggested by Sally Edwards, winner of the 1993 Iditashoe race in Alaska. Run for two minutes, walk briskly for four; repeat. If that's too easy, use a 1:1 ratio — two minutes running, two minutes fast walking. You'll get a good workout, even if you don't run at the same speed you do on the roads or trails.

You might even consider entering a snowshoe race. Country parks and other recreational areas often sponsor such

How to survive winter

Training isn't a fair-weather activity — it's something you do on a regular basis, even during the winter.

You'll feel the cold most during the first few days of wintry weather. After a few weeks, your body will accommodate the lower temperatures by producing more heat. But if you are to become accustomed to the cold, you must exercise in the cold. Here are some guidelines for your winter workouts:

NEVER PUSH YOURSELF TO EXHAUSTION

While you should exercise at a high enough intensity to maintain your core temperature, you don't want to overdo it.

While cycling, your body will generate eight to 12 times the heat that it would while at rest. Under most circumstances, if you are properly dressed, cold weather will have little or no effect on your body temperature because your energy production overrides the cold temperatures and wind chill.

However, you may become tired sooner. Riding a heavier bicycle, coupled with the added wind drag and weight of more clothing and heavier shoes, will increase your energy expenditure. So be certain to conserve plenty of energy for emergencies and unexpected weather conditions.

WATCH THE WIND

Exercise into the wind on the way out, and with the wind at your back on the way home. The wind will help you when you are tired at the end of the workout, so you won't slow down and get chilled.

DRESS PROPERLY

Wear a cover on top of your helmet and a knit cap under it; the best kind converts into a face mask that can extend to cover your neck. You can lose up to 40 percent of your body heat from your head and neck if they are not properly protected. If you're riding into the wind, pull the cap down over your face for extra protection.

Dress in layers — insulating fabrics that wick moisture away from the skin, and "breathable" outer garments. You should be able to stay warm and dry on the most miserable day.

Wear mittens, not gloves. Mittens trap all of the hand's warmth in a single compartment. Wear a pair of thin, full-fingered liners underneath your mittens to promote extra warmth.

Use shoe covers, wear heavy socks, and try to use all-leather, mountain-bike shoes with clipless pedals.

WORK OUT WHEN IT'S WARM OUT

Exercise during the midday. The sunlight will help you stay warmer during the day; it will be easier for drivers to see you in daylight; and it will be easier for you to watch the surfaces you are riding on for snow, ice or puddles.

REMEMBER TO EAT AND DRINK

While you don't need to dramatically increase your calorie intake during winter exercise, consider eating a snack before your ride. Digestion will add some heat to your body and help keep you warm.

Fluid replacement, however, is crucial. There are three times when an athlete training in the winter should drink: when he or she is thirsty, when he or she isn't thirsty, and in between.

Why? Cold air must be warmed and moistened in your throat and lungs. As you exhale, you lose lots of water, which is why you can see your breath during heavy exercise. Urine production also increases in cold weather.

Dehydration can lead to fatigue, which will affect your ability to train or compete at your optimum. Worse yet, a serious decrease in your blood volume will reduce blood flow to your skin and extremities — this will cause your body to cool more rapidly, and can lead to hypothermia and/or frostbite.

Carry your fluids under your jacket and close to your body to keep it from getting too cold. A CamelBak hydration system is an excellent choice to wear under your jacket. Use energy drinks that contain carbohydrate — they will do double duty, replacing carbohydrate and fluid. Drink 8 to 12 ounces before your ride, and 4 to 8 ounces every 15 to 20 minutes while exercising.

Avoid drinks containing caffeine and alcohol; they speed up dehydration by promoting urine production. Alcohol also decreases glucose output by the liver in the cold, and speeds heat loss by dilating your skin's blood vessels.

RIDE SMART

Your hat and helmet cover may cut down on your hearing and visual acuity, so be more cautious about cars approaching you from behind. Ride defensively and cautiously.

BEWARE OF HYPOTHERMIA

One of the most common and serious cold-weather injuries is hypothermia, in which the body's core temperature starts to drop. Brought on by a combination of fatigue, damp clothing and wind chill, hypothermia's early signs include shivering, muscle weakness and loss of coordination.

It needn't be very cold for hypothermia to set in, either. Cyclists who do not ventilate

properly, wear cotton undergarments, and then slow down for some reason, can begin to lose heat rapidly .

The best thing you can do to avoid hypothermia is to keep cycling and get the wind to your back. If you stop riding, get indoors. As soon as the ride is over, head into the house, take a warm shower and put on dry clothes.

A useful mnemonic to use during winter cycling is VIP: Ventilate, Insulate and Protect:

• Ventilate excess water perspiration.

• Insulate, particularly high blood flow areas such as the neck and head.

• Protect from wind and wetness with appropriate clothing.

WINTER MOUNTAIN BIKING

Want to keep on riding all winter? While many cyclists only venture outdoors when the roads and trails are dry, others are finding that winter mountain biking offers some of the hardest riding of the year — it's every bit as challenging as a summer single-track ride.

Simon Rakower of All Weather Sports in Fairbanks,

Alaska, is the foremost expert on the sport. He runs a business that caters to winter cycling and has a site on the internet (http://www.mosquitonet.com/~aws) that offers a multitude of information on training, equipment and events for those wanting to learn more about winter cycling.

Rakower calls snow riding "more interesting and fun than riding on the dirt." And talk about power riding — wait till you go on your first ride in four to six inches of powder. It's hard and technical; 10 miles in snow is like 20 miles on dirt.

EQUIPMENT

"You don't need a fancy bike with dual suspension and hydraulic brakes," Rakower says. But you might try a few modifications to your summertime steed.

Try using Snow Cat's double-wide rims with 26x2.2 tires front and rear, with 10 to 15 pounds of pressure. While most good wide tires with a mud pattern will work in the snow, if you're riding on ice you may want to get a set of Nokian metal stud tires, which will help greatly on ice but not on snow. Both are available from All Weather Sports at 907/474-8184.

Replace your clipless pedals with standard pedals and add extra-large Power Grips to the pedals so you can ride in hiking boots. Use a personal-hydration system for carrying your water or sports drink; wear it under your jacket so the water does not freeze.

TECHNIQUE

Mastering snow cycling won't just make you a good snow rider. You will develop an enhanced feel for your bike and an increased sense of balance that will serve you year round.

Some cyclists just don't believe how easy it is to cycle outdoors with your snow-equipped mountain bike. If you're such a disbeliever, think back to your first long ride as a cyclist. You probably thought 25 miles was a long, hard distance to ride. It can be, until you have worked up to that distance, but once you've been there, it's much

easier the next time out.
  Cycling in the cold and snow is similar. It seems difficult until you do it. Then it gets easier every time. The winter season isn't a frigid torture chamber; it's just another season in your yearly training program. And training isn't a fair-weather activity. It's something you do on a regular basis, week-in and week-out.
  Jeep trails, ski area access roads, old mining roads and snowmobile trails are ideal for riding. Stay away from groomed cross-country ski trails. If you try to pedal in more than four or five inches of powder with your standard

wheels, you'll sink in like you are standing in quicksand. Hardpack is best; packed powder is great. Packed hardpack with a few inches of powder and you'll think you're riding on top of the clouds.
  The secret to riding in the snow is flotation and slow, steady movements. Maintain a slow and steady rhythm; ride at a slightly lower cadence and higher gear than you normally would; and do not jump too hard out of the saddle when you need to accelerate. Steer with smooth and wide turns, and if the bike wants to slip in on one direction, then let it.

events. Check with the sporting-goods retailers in your area, or your regional outdoor-sports publication, to find out where events are taking place.

Snowshoe training is deceptive. It looks easy, but it's packed with cardiovascular intensity. That's the beauty of this winter sport, which combines technical simplicity with lung-busting exercise for an excellent workout package. It's hard work, but as the winter turns to spring, the lactic acid eases and your form will be excellent.

CHAPTER EIGHT

Stretching

"When I say rest, I don't mean lying on the beach drinking beer. Rest is rest from the bike, not rest from training."
— Eddie Borysewicz,
Former national cycling coach

As we have seen, good physical performance is based on strength, power and endurance. But there is a fourth important component that many cyclists overlook — flexibility.

Increased flexibility can be achieved by adding stretching to your fitness program. Stretching is also highly recommended by the American College of Sports Medicine.

As you ride, row, step or strength-train on resistance equipment, your muscles become stronger, but tighter. You may experience tightness and pain in the lower back, hamstrings, or shoulders. This is a warning sign that you are experiencing a gradual loss of muscle elasticity and a decrease in joint flexibility. Stretching, which requires no special skill, can relieve this condition, aid recovery and help prevent soreness.

Stretching before your workout will help circulate more blood through your muscles and prepare them for the hard work to come. Stretching between exercises (or when you change pieces of equipment) will help relieve muscle tension and may help postpone fatigue. Stretching after your workout will help you cool down and may prevent some soreness.

Technique

A long, sustained, stretch — called a static stretch — is a far superior method of stretching your muscles and surrounding connective tissue than bouncing, or ballistic stretching. An easy static stretch should be done without any feeling of pain that can be associated with other types of stretching technique.

Get used to feeling an "easy" stretch, a stretch that feels good, for 15-30 seconds. If you stretch correctly, maintain the easy stretch for enough time, the result will be less tension in the muscles you are stretching. The result will be increased flexibility, an essential component of your overall fitness.

Stretching exercises

Below is a 10-minute program that can be done before, after or even during your workout. These same stretches can also be used during the cycling season to aid with stiffness you may experience after a long, hard ride. The following stretches come from *Stretching* by Bob Anderson.

Elongation

Straighten out your arms and legs. Point your fingers and toes as you stretch as far as you can. Stretch and then relax. Hold for five seconds. This is a good stretch for the entire body.

Achilles and calf stretch

The back leg should start out straight with the foot flat and

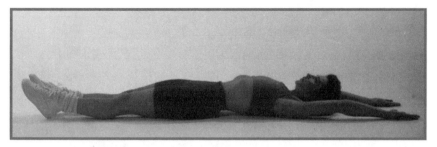

[ELONGATION]

[ACHILLES AND CALF STRETCH]   [STANDING QUADS]

pointing straight ahead, then slightly bend the back knee, still keeping the foot flat. This gives you a much lower stretch, which is also good for maintaining or regaining ankle flexibility. Hold 15 seconds each leg. This area needs only a slight feeling of stretch.

Standing quads

Hold top of left foot (from inside of foot) with right hand and gently pull heel toward buttocks. Stretch both legs.

Shoulder stretch

To stretch the back of the arms, shoulders and waist, gently pull your elbow behind your head as you slowly lean to the side until a mild stretch is felt. Hold stretch for 10 seconds. Stretch both shoulders.

[SHOULDER STRETCH]

Williams flex stretch

Straighten both legs and relax, then pull your right leg toward your chest. For this stretch keep the back of your head on the mat, if possible, but do not strain. Repeat with your left leg.

Hamstring

Further stretches the hamstrings and calf. Lie on floor and bend your left knee, keeping your back flat on the floor. Lift right leg straight up and from the hip and then lower it, hold for 10

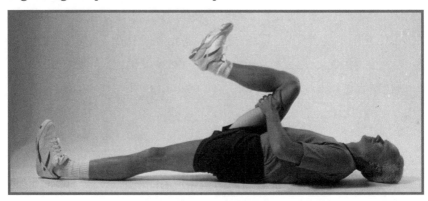

[WILLIAMS FLEX STRETCH]

[HAMSTRING]

[SITTING GROIN]

[SPRINTER'S STRETCH]

to 15 seconds. Use your hands if you need help.

Sitting groin

Put the soles of your feet together with your heels a comfortable distance from your groin. Put your hands around your feet and slowly pull yourself forward until you feel an easy stretch in the groin. Make your movement forward by bending from the hips and not from the shoulders.

Sprinter's stretch

Move one leg forward until the knee of the forward leg is directly over the ankle. Your other knee should be resting on the floor. Now, without changing the position of the knee on the floor or the forward foot, lower the front of your hip downward to create an easy stretch. This will help relieve tension in the lower back.

SUMMARY

It is easy to forgo stretching, but it is as important to your overall fitness as your strength and aerobic conditioning. Stretching can also serve as relaxation time, which is also beneficial to your overall health and well-being.

It should only take a few minutes to stretch properly before and after you exercise. This small expenditure of time can keep injuries and tightness to a minimum. As you stretch, you learn about your body and how it moves and feels. You also learn how to take care of your body to prevent injury and excess tension. Stretching is a great form of physical education.

AFTERWORD

Best of luck with your off-season. Your investment in a well-planned exercise program will prepare you for upcoming events and help you reach your physical potential.

Remember not to feel too guilty about not being on your bike four to six times per week during the off-season. The other aerobic activities we've discussed will keep you in top form; prevent you from getting stale; and make you a better cyclist. The benefits cross-training provides cannot be denied, and, once discovered, cannot be ignored.

Enjoy your off-season training, and I will see you on the road in the spring.

SUGGESTED READING

Anderson, Bob. *Stretching*, Bolinas, CA, 1980: Shelter Publications, Inc.

Baker, Arnie. *Smart Cycling: Training and Racing for Riders of All Levels*, New York, 1997: Simon & Schuster. 800/223-2348.

Baker, Arnie. *Bicycling Medicine: Bicycling Health, Fitness, and Injury Explained*, New York: 1998, Simon & Schuster. 800/223-2348, Before May 1998, San Diego: Argo Publishing. 619/295-7632.

Baker, Arnie. *The Essential Cyclist*, New York, 1998: Lyons & Burford. 800/836-0510.

Burke, Edmund. *Serious Cycling*, Champaign, IL, 1996: Human Kinetics Publishers.

Burke, Edmund. *The Complete Home Fitness Handbook*, Champaign, IL, 1996: Human Kinetics Publishers.

Burney, Simon. *Cyclo-cross*, Boulder, CO, 1996: VeloPress. 800/234-8356.

Chu, Don. *Jumping into Plyometrics*, Champaign, IL, 1992: Human Kinetics Publishers.

Matheny, Fred and Stephen Grabe. *Weight Training for Cyclists*, Brattleboro, VT, 1986: Velo-news.

Conditioning Press. *Performance Conditioning for Cycling*. Lincoln, NE. A newsletter that contains information on off-season conditioning directed to the cyclist. 800/578-4636

Videotape:

Newton, Harvey. *Strength Training for Cyclists*. Newton Sports, PO Box 2595, Colorado Springs, CO 80910-2595.

INDEX

149

151

153

155

OTHER BOOKS FROM VELOPRESS

Cyclist's Training Bible *by Joe Friel*
Now in its third printing! Hailed as a major breakthrough in training for competitive cycling, this book helps take cyclists from where they are to where they want to be — the podium. • 288 pp. • Photos, charts, diagrams • Paperback • **1-884737-21-8** • **P-BIB $19.95**

Single-Track Mind *by Paul Skilbeck*
This book represents a quantum leap in mountain-bike training guides — the right combination of scientific training information, bike-handling skills, nutrition, mental training, and a proven year-round training plan. • 128 pp. • Photos, charts, diagrams • Paperback • **1-884737-10-2** • **P-STM $19.95**

Cyclo-cross *by Simon Burney*
A must read for anyone brave enough to ride their road bike downhill through the mud. Expanded from the original to include mountain-bike conversion to cyclo-cross. • 200 pp. • Photos, charts, diagrams • Paperback • **1-884737-20-X** • **P-CRS $19.95**

The Mountain Biker's Cookbook *by Jill Smith*
Healthy and delicious recipes from the world's best mountain-bike racers. The ideal marriage between calories and the perfect way to burn them off. • 152 pp. • Paperback • **1-884737-23-4** • **P-EAT $14.95**

VeloNews Training Diary *by Joe Friel*
The world's most popular training diary for cyclists. Allows you to record every facet of training with plenty of room for notes. Non-dated, so you can start any time of the year. • 235 pp. • Spiral-bound • **1-884737-42-0** • **P-DIA $12.95**

Inside Triathlon Training Diary *by Joe Friel*
The best multisport diary available anywhere. Combines the best in quantitative and qualitative training notation. Designed to help you attain your best fitness ever. Non-dated, so you can start at any time of the year. • 235 pp. • Spiral-bound • **1-884737-41-2** • **P-IDI $12.95**

Barnett's Manual *by John Barnett*
The most expensive bicycle maintenance manual in the world ... and worth every penny. Regarded by professionals worldwide as the final word in bicycle maintenance. • 950 pp. • Illustrations, diagrams, charts • Five-ring loose-leaf binder. • **1-884737-16-1** • **P-BNT $149.95**

Bicycle Racing in the Modern Era *from the editors of* VeloNews
These 63 articles represent the best in cycling journalism over the past quarter century: the world championships (road and mountain), the Tour de France, technical innovations and much, much more. • 218 pp. • Paperback. • **1-884737-32-3** • **P-MOD $19.95**

Half-Wheel Hell *by Maynard Hershon*
This collection from writer Maynard Hershon gives a human view of cycling and the culture that surrounds it. Hershon explores our perception of ourselves and our sport with humor and sensitivity. • 134 pp. • Paperback • **1-884737-05-6** • **P-HWH $13.95**

Tour de France THE 75TH ANNIVERSARY BICYCLE RACE *by Robin Magowan*
A masterful account of the 1978 Tour de France, the Tour's 75th anniversary. Magowan's fluid prose style brings to life the most contested Tour de France as if it were yesterday. • 208 pp. • Photos and stage profiles • Hardbound • **1-884737-13-7** • **P-MAG $24.95**

Tales from the Toolbox *by Scott Parr with Rupert Guinness*
In his years as a Motorola team mechanic, Scott Parr saw it all. *Tales from the Toolbox* takes you inside the Motorola team van on the roads of Europe. Get the inside dirt on the pro peloton and the guys who really make it happen ... the mechanics, of course. • 168 pp. • Paperback • **1-884737-39-0** • **P-TFT $14.95**

Eddy Merckx *by Rik Vanwalleghem*
Discover the passion and fear that motivated the world's greatest cyclist. The man they called "the cannibal" is captured like never before in this lavish coffee-table book. • 216 pp. • 24 color & 165 B/W photos • Hardback • **1-884737-22-6** • **P-EDY $49.95**

Bobke *by Bob Roll*
If Hunter S. Thompson and Dennis Rodman had a boy, he would write like Bob Roll: rough-hewn, poetic gonzo. Roll's been there and has the T-shirts to prove it. If you like straight talk, or cycling, or both, this book is a must read. • 124 pp. • Photos • Paperback • **1-884737-12-9** • **P-BOB $16.95**

A Season in Turmoil *by Samuel Abt*
Samuel Abt traces the differing fortunes of American road racers Lance Armstrong and Greg LeMond through the 1994 season. With revealing, in-depth interviews, Abt examines the raw exuberance of Armstrong as he becomes the top U.S. road cycling star, while LeMond sinks toward an unwanted retirement. • 178 pp. • B/W photos • Paperback • **1-884737-09-9** • **P-SIT $14.95**

Zinn & the Art of Mountain Bike Maintenance *by Lennard Zinn*
Regardless of your mountain-bike experience or mechanical prowess, Zinn will guide you through every aspect of mountain-bike maintenance, repair and troubleshooting in a succinct, idiot-proof format. Exploded diagrams and easy-to-follow instructions for everything from flat repair to wheel building. • 288 pp • Illustrations • Paperback • **1-884737-47-1** • **P-ZIN $17.95**

For ordering or more information, please call VeloPress toll-free:

800/234-8356

ABOUT THE AUTHOR

Edmund R. Burke, Ph.D., is a professor at the University of Colorado at Colorado Springs. He is the author of *Serious Cycling, Training Nutrition, High-Tech Cycling and Precision Heart Rate Training*, and serves on the fitness advisory board for *Bicycling* magazine. He was a staff member with the 1980 and 1984 U.S. Olympic cycling teams, and coordinator of Project '96 for the 1996 Olympic Games.